KEYS TO BUILDING A GREAT CHURCH

ABOUT THIS BOOK

"*How can we build a great church?*" is a question that is asked by church leaders probably more than any other, and is probably the hardest to answer fully. This book has been written as a resource for leaders, to pass on the experience and wisdom gained by the authors over many years of service in God's Kingdom and in building His Church, in the hope of answering that question.

This book provides a tried-and-tested framework for developing a healthy, thriving church capable of expanding the Kingdom and reaching souls for the Lord whilst maintaining balance in the lives of the leaders. It is an essential manual for learning how to build a strong and effective church with an atmosphere of joy and love for the Lord.

About The Authors

Colin Cooper

Colin became a Christian at the age of 18 and was ordained a Pastor in the Assemblies of God in his 30s. He was part of the Home Missions Team planting churches in un-reached areas of Britain and now lives in Huddersfield where he is the Senior Pastor of Huddersfield Christian Fellowship.

He is married to Sue, has 2 children and 5 grandchildren (so far!)

Colin is the leader of MFE (Ministers Fellowship Europe) which is part of Ministers Fellowship International.

As well as having a heart for Europe, he also travels extensively in Africa, India, the USA and Canada. He has a heart to see lives changed by the power of the Holy Spirit and people growing in God. In fact – Colin just has a heart for people!

Sierd De Jong

Sierd has been brought up in a Christian home and at the age of 12 he chose personally to dedicate his life to God. He already had a desire to work for God. In his home church he served as a cell group leader, youth leader and later became one of the elders. It was in May 1996 that Sierd and Mirjam were sent out to start a church and pastor in a village called Zevenhuizen (The Netherlands).

Sierd and Mirjam have 3 daughters and are also part of the MFE leadership team. Sierd has a heart to see strong local churches being built so they can be a strong testimony for the Lord Jesus Christ and produce lasting fruit.

GORDON TOSE

Gordon joined Huddersfield Christian Fellowship and its Pastor, Colin Cooper, in 1988, three years after becoming a Christian.

He came onto the church staff in 1991, became an elder in 1993 and since then has developed a real understanding of how the local church functions. His particular areas of interest are church government, support leadership and relationships generally and has taught extensively on these subjects both in the UK and abroad.

Gordon is married to Marjorie and has two sons, both of whom are part of the Fellowship.

CHIP KAWALSINGH

Chip is the Senior Pastor of Harvest City Church in Leicester, England and is a regular speaker at churches and conferences worldwide. He is a graduate of Portland Bible College in Portland, Oregon, USA.

He and his wife Sarah also serve on the leadership team of MFE, and have two children, Brandon & Dylan.

Chip is the author of several books, including *God, a Mocha & Me*, *Formation Leadership* and the *Partnership Guide*.

MEMOS SAKELLARIOU

Memos has been pastoring since 1979 and has been the Senior Pastor of a thriving, growing church in Athens, Greece since 1988.

He and his wife Efi were married in 1977 and have one son, two daughters and one grandson (so far!).

Memos has a heart to reach out to other local Greek pastors.

ABOUT MINISTERS FELLOWSHIP EUROPE

Ministers Fellowship Europe (MFE) is an organisation which supports pastors and elders and is based on relationships. It is the European expression of Ministers Fellowship International (MFI) which is based in Portland, Oregon USA.

MFE exists to facilitate and nurture meaningful relationships amongst members, equipping and enabling them to be more effective in their calling, for the purpose of building and multiplying strong local churches around the world.

MFE aims to support church leaders by helping them to establish meaningful covenant relationships with like-minded leaders, by providing resources to the ministers to enhance their personal life and ministry, by providing a sense of covering and accountability, by providing for the rejuvenation and refreshing of battle-weary leaders and by giving each member a sense of connection to a larger family network and a worldwide vision.

MFE benefits congregations by assisting their pastors and leaders, giving congregations a sense of national and international identity, providing a sense of security and a place to turn in times of difficulty, and by exposing local congregations to ministries that will build what they are building.

If you would like to learn more about MFE, please contact us:

Ministers Fellowship Europe   T: +44 (0)1484 467324
Cathedral House   F: +44 (0)1484 467325
Huddersfield
HD1 3LG   info@ministersfellowshipeurope.org
United Kingdom   **www.ministersfellowshipeurope.org**

KEYS TO BUILDING A
GREAT CHURCH

COLIN COOPER – SIERD DE JONG – GORDON TOSE
CHIP KAWALSINGH – MEMOS SAKELLARIOU

FOREWORD BY DR. DICK IVERSON

ISBN 978-0-9561415-1-4
A catalogue record for this book is available from the British Library

First published in the UK in 2009 by Harvest City Publishing
www.harvestcitypublishing.com

Edited By Paul Goffin, Nicola Holmes, Sue Cooper & Darrell Woods
Cover Design by Marcus Woolcock

Printed in Great Britain by the MPG Books Group, Bodmin and King's Lynn

www.harvestcitypublishing.com

Table Of Contents

FOREWORD

In Matthew 16:18 Jesus tells us "I will build my church; and the gates of hell shall not prevail against it." Yes, Jesus *is* building His Church, but He is using you and me to do it.

Acts 20:28 tells us how precious the Church is to our Lord in that He purchased it with his own blood. It's a wonderful and amazing thing that He has entrusted us with the honour and responsibility of caring for and feeding that flock.

You hold in your hands a manual that summarizes the primary keys that will bring life, strength, health, and balance to the local church. I am confident that as you follow the principles of this book, which are rooted in the Bible, that you will experience the joy of a healthy, growing church.

I have the privilege of knowing all the contributors and they are well qualified to author such a book. May God bless you as you read this book and walk in the truths that are shared.

DICK IVERSON

CHAIRMAN

MINISTERS FELLOWSHIP INTERNATIONAL

Chapter 1 – Colin Cooper

Building and Growing a Great Church

How to grow a great church is a question that comes up and is asked probably more than any other. When asked this particular question I have not been able to answer with a short sentence, but there are ingredients which are indispensable in building a great, growing church where there is excitement, joy and anticipation for the next service with the saints.

These ingredients are (in no particular order):

Ingredient 1 – Quality Control Is Vital

Matthew 4:24 tells us that large crowds followed Jesus and things were happening. Wow! This looked like revival! As the people saw healings and miracles His fame spread; what would you give to have a church growing in revival like this? But wait a minute, let's take stock of all this. Later, Jesus was left with a handful of men; in fact only 120 were in the upper room. What happened to the thousands? Most followed Jesus because of what He was doing. Excitement draws the crowds but it's impossible to build with them long term because they follow with the condition that you keep producing the action. But when the action stops so the crowds stop coming. It is far better to have 50 people who are with you than 1000 who are not. You will go further with a quality, faithful 50 than conditional relationships of 1000s.

INGREDIENT 2 – LOOSE JOINTS

Eph 4:16 talks about being joined together. Crowds are loose joints. How do we know if we have loose joints? Change something in the church. A loose joint will react, but a firm joint will respond. Loose joints are exactly that, loose; so they leave the church more easily. Here are some principles that will help you spot a loose joint:

    a. Secret accusations.

    b. Distrust your motives.

    c. Suspicious of Biblical accuracy (where does it say that?).

    d. Seek advice outside the house.

    e. What <u>you do</u> in this church rather than what <u>we do.</u>

It's impossible to grow a great church with loose joints; they have to be jointed in and joined to you if a church is to grow to be great.

INGREDIENT 3 – ABILITY IS SECONDARY

Ability can be a reason why some churches are not growing and are not great. David's son Absalom had ability and people liked him - 2 Samuel 15:13. So he had ability but God wasn't in that ability. Our souls can do anything the Spirit can, except give lasting life.

    a. Does God come down in what he does?

    b. Is he trustworthy?

    c. Does he finish what he started? Proverbs 18:9.

    d. Can he receive correction? Proverbs 12:1 states if we can't take correction then we are stupid. Wow! Strong words! Jesus taught those who would listen, not those who were speaking.

    e. Does he serve? Doing menial tasks not just platform ones.

    f. Does he have integrity with his words and actions? Often insecurity is in an individual's life when there is a lack of integrity. Proverbs 10:9, 11:3.

INGREDIENT 4 - FAITHFULNESS

1 Corinthians 4:2 - proved faithful when given trust; a great church is filled with faithful people. Proverbs 28:20 says, "a faithful man is full of blessing".

I have seen leaders give roles or jobs in the church either to keep people or encourage them. Never do this because either they will leave later in the midst of their responsibility or you have to keep encouraging continually. If you want a job done give it to a busy man. Matthew 13:12 says give to him who has. A faithful man is already doing jobs; unfaithful men find it easier to do things for Jesus than to listen to Him. The unfaithful are destroyed by their duplicity - Proverbs 11:3. So you cannot build with men who are destroying themselves.

An ingredient of a growing church that brings favour. A good name in the sight of God and also to men is fierce faithfulness. Proverbs 3:3-4 spells this out.

INGREDIENT 5 – DON'T GRAB PEOPLE

Many of us try to grab people in order to grow a church. Yet scripture warns us against doing that. Nehemiah 7:3 is a good example. Remember the Old Testament is a shadow of the New, what's revealed in the New is concealed in the Old. The city here reflects the Church - and Nehemiah gave this instruction 'Do not open the gates of the city until the sun comes up' - why did he say this?

In the dark you could not see what men were bringing into the city in their carts. But when the sun came up it shone down into the carts and revealed anything harmful to the city. In the New Testament Paul warns us in Acts 20:28–30 to guard the flock from wolves; the shepherd would lie across the door of the sheep pen so nothing got in or out without him being in control and aware.

As leaders we should guard what comes into our city, the Church, until we find out what is in their cart or heart. One way to do this is to have a course teaching the spirit of your church, i.e. start from the basics: water baptism, repentance, Holy Spirit, how you function as a government in the house, family, discipleship, fellowship, finances, worship, gifts, what the church is, membership, what the body is, discipline in church and other subjects which would be the heart and spirit of your church. Some will drop out when they are taught about beliefs they are not happy with.

It will save heartache and a war in the future.

This guards the church, so you are not left with quantity but quality and you will go further and build better with quality. In practice we have found that only a tiny minority drop out, but they are a little yeast you can do without.

1 Corinthians 5:6 - A little yeast works through the whole batch of dough.
Luke 13:21 - A woman took the yeast and mixed it into the flour, it worked through the dough.

So in spite of the temptation do not grab people. Jesus understood this ingredient better than anyone. He said, "I will only have what the Father gives" - John 6:3 - and that's the best way to grow a great church - 1 Corinthians 3:10 says, "be careful how you build".

INGREDIENT 6 – BUILDING WITH AUTHORITY

Most problems in church are to do with authority. When I first entered the ministry I really wanted and tried to be liked, but it caused me to abdicate my God given authority. In turn this made problems in the saints and sinners more acute, until one day I sensed the Lord gently say, "Colin you are not in a popularity contest". Wow! I woke up to my calling.

Authority is in all of life – I am glad when flying that the final authority is with the pilot and not the passengers. When I am in a dimly lit street and I see an unhealthy group of hooligans, I am relieved when a policeman steps out of a car and uses his authority. Jesus Himself submitted to authority - "not My will but Yours" He said to God - Luke 22:42. As leaders the buck stops with you and it's called accountability. Where real authority is exercised, the flock of that church is always very secure because they know, whether good or bad, things will be dealt with in a Biblical manner. This is an ingredient for a secure, happy, growing church.

We must learn to settle for respect rather than the need to be liked.

INGREDIENT 7 – BUILDING WITH CHARACTER

People can be like apples. There is a worm that lives on the apple blossom, and when the apple forms it grows around the worm. Then the worm leaves the rotten core and eats its way out of the apple, leaving a hole. Most people think it's the worm eating into the apple. That's just like us; it's not what goes into a man that defiles, but what comes out of him. Jesus said in Matthew 15:11-18, "it's the things that come out of the heart".

Leaders look on the outward appearance of man - he looks good, speaks well and preaches with excellence, so we put him on the platform. But we have not seen what his spirit is like. Is he rebellious? With a history of broken relationships? And even adulterous? Ultimately he hurts the church and we can't build with him because his character cannot go where his gift has taken him.

To build a great church, men with good character are indispensable; in fact you will build a better church with a man who has limited gift and ability but excellent character than with a man who has a great gift and personality but a bad character.

CONCLUSION

So the ingredients needed to build a great, growing church:

1. Quality control is vital.
2. Being jointed together.
3. More than just ability.
4. Absolute faithfulness.
5. Not grabbing people.
6. Build with authority.
7. Build with character.

These ingredients not only build a great church, but help the leader to enjoy the journey and have fun with those he works alongside. These ingredients will also prevent burnout, breakdown and depression.

Chapter 2 – Sierd De Jong

Building Strong and Secure Churches

Introduction

First of all I need to say that a lot of the ideas and concepts that are in this chapter and in the chapters on structure and accountability in this book I have drawn from material that brother Kevin Conner provided when he gave a seminar in our church many years ago. The teachings on the Church from Brother Kevin Conner have been a great blessing to us and have become part of my own convictions as a Pastor. All the information that was taught in that seminar and that has become part of my belief system came out when I started writing these chapters.

There have been many Christians who were willing and available to be used by God who have put their time, talents, money and energy into all kinds of activities outside the context of the local church. After many years they look back and wonder if all the effort they have put in has produced the lasting fruits for the Kingdom of God which they desired.

God has shown us in His word how lasting results for the Kingdom of God can be achieved. The title of this chapter already gives us the answer to this question; it is by building strong and secure churches.

WHY STRONG AND SECURE CHURCHES?

Ephesians 3:10-11 (NIV) - [10] His intent was that now, *through the church*, the manifold wisdom of God should be made known to the rulers and authorities in the heavenly realms, [11] according to His eternal purpose which he accomplished in Christ Jesus our Lord.

To understand the importance of building strong and secure churches, we need to understand the role the Church has to play in the purposes of God. God's overall purpose is to establish and extend His Kingdom on the Earth. That is that His will is being done and His rule is being established in the hearts and lives of people and through them in their families, communities, nations and continents.

However, a purpose needs an instrument in order to become a reality and God has used different instruments through the ages to fulfil His purpose. In his book *The Church in the New Testament*, Brother Kevin Conner explains that through the ages God progressively used different instruments. The following thoughts are taken in brief from his book.

1. **Adam and Eve**

    The original instruments were Adam and Eve. The Kingdom of God was given to them and they were called to rule over creation and subdue it (Gen. 1:26-28). By falling in sin, they failed to fulfil their calling to be an instrument through which the kingdom of God would be established on the Earth.

2. **The Patriarchs**

    Men like Noah, Abraham, Isaac and Jacob were called to be instruments through which the will of God was done on the Earth. Although they were not perfect they knew God's rule in their lives and they were part of the lineage through which the Lord Jesus would come.

3. **Israel**

    At a certain time God called Israel out of all the other nations. Israel was a nation under God's rule and God intended that through them other nations would see God's glory, might and rule so that other nations would have a revelation of the only true God (Ex. 19:6). Saul, David and Solomon reigned as kings over a united nation, but after Solomon the nation was split into two parts - the house of Israel and the house of Judah (1 Kings 11-12; Ezek. 16, 23).

Both houses gave themselves over to idolatry. This became so bad that God allowed both houses to be taken into captivity and they failed to be an instrument of the Kingdom of God.

4. **The Lord Jesus Christ**

After restoring the house of Judah back to the land, the Lord Jesus Christ, the King Himself, came. It was through Him that God ruled on the earth. Through the ministry of the Lord Jesus Christ, that is by preaching, teaching the gospel of the Kingdom and by demonstrating the Kingdom through the healing of the sick and the deliverance of people from evil spirits, the Kingdom of God came among men (Matt. 4:23; 12:28; Mark 1:14; Luke 11:20; Acts 1:3). Jesus taught that this gospel of the Kingdom would be preached over the entire world (Matt. 24:14).

The majority of the Jews in the days of the Lord Jesus rejected Him because they expected Jesus to restore a national and a natural Kingdom. When He did not do this they rejected Him. God then took the Kingdom from them and gave it to another people.

Matthew 21:43 (NIV) - [43]Therefore I tell you that the kingdom of God will be taken away from you and given to a people who will produce its fruit.

5. **The Church**

The people to whom the Kingdom was given, and through whom the Kingdom is being revealed, were the Church which consisted of believing Jews and Gentiles (Eph. 2:11-16). This was God's eternal purpose (Eph. 3:10-11). Before time began, in eternity past, God already intended to have a people out of every nation, tribe and tongue, to unite them in Christ and to use them as His instrument to demonstrate the Kingdom of God on the Earth (1 Pet. 2:9-10).

The early Church was strong and effective. This church reached the whole of the then known world with the gospel of the Kingdom (Acts 17:6; 24:5; Rom. 1:8), but through the ages the Church lost its power and its effectiveness. Although the Church did decline it will not fail, because the Lord Jesus Christ is building His Church and He will not fail (Matt. 16:18). He is restoring His Church to become a strong, overcoming and glorious church in order for the Church to become all that God had intended her to be (Eph. 5:25-27).

WHAT MAKES A CHURCH STRONG AND SECURE?

When the Lord Jesus ascended to heaven, He gave leadership ministries to the Church through which He is building His Church. The leaders have the task of building wisely and correctly in order for the Church to be strong and secure (Eph. 4:11-16; 1 Cor. 3:10-15).

Proverbs 24:3 (NIV) - 3 By wisdom a house is built, and through understanding it is established.

The Bible teaches that the fear of God is the beginning of wisdom (Ps. 111:10; Prov. 1:7; 9:10). The fear of God means that we realise the need to obey God otherwise we will suffer the consequences. The Church must be built according to His pattern, which He has laid down for us in His word, in order to become the instrument that will have an impact and produce lasting results. In this chapter we are going to take a closer look at God's pattern for His Church to help us see what makes a church strong and secure.

1 Timothy 3:15 (NKJV) - 15 but if I am delayed, I write so that you may know how you ought to conduct yourself in the house of God, which is the church of the living God, the pillar and ground of the truth.

As we can see in this scripture the Bible compares the Church to a house. A strong and secure house basically consists of three things:

a. A good foundation.
b. A good structure.
c. A good roof.

We can also see these three things in the following passage:

Matthew 7:24-28 (NKJV) - 24 "Therefore whoever hears these sayings of Mine, and does them, I will liken him to a wise man who built his house on the rock: 25 and the rain descended, the floods came, and the winds blew and beat on that house; and it did not fall, for it was founded on the rock. 26 "But everyone who hears these sayings of Mine, and does not do them, will be like a foolish man who built his house on the sand: 27 and the rain descended, the floods came, and the winds blew and beat on that house; and it fell. And great was its fall."

We read that the storm which tested the house consisted of a flood, a wind and rain. This indicates that besides a strong foundation, a house also needs a good structure and a good roof.

The flood tested the foundation, the wind tested the structure and the rain tested the roof. Every church can expect the same tests and by them we can see if it is built correctly.

In this chapter we are going to look at the importance of a good foundation. In chapters three and eleven we are going to look at the importance of a good structure and roof.

The Importance of a Good Foundation

> Psalm 11:3 (NIV) - 3 When the foundations are being destroyed, what can the righteous do?

Just as you cannot build a solid and secure house without a good foundation, neither can you build a strong and secure church without a good and solid foundation.

What is a Solid Foundation for the Church?

The foundation of the Church is threefold.

1. **The Lord Jesus Christ.**

   > 1 Corinthians 3:10-11 (NKJV) - 10 According to the grace of God which was given to me, as a wise master builder I have laid the foundation, and another builds on it. But let each one take heed how he builds on it. 11 For no other foundation can anyone lay than that which is laid, which is Jesus Christ.

   That the Lord Jesus Christ is the foundation of the Church means:

   a. All that **the Lord Jesus is**. He is the Son of God and He is the only Way to God (Acts 9:20; John 14:6). When churches start to challenge the Biblical view of whom the Lord Jesus is they start to undermine their own foundation.

   b. All that **He has said**. The Lord Jesus said that the words He spoke were not His own, but of His Father (John 5:19). We must not speak our own words, but the words of the Lord Jesus Christ. This will strengthen the foundation of the Church.

c. All that **He has done**. This especially concerns the death, burial and resurrection of the Lord Jesus Christ (1 Cor. 2:2; 15; Gal. 6:14). All we are and all we do as churches is because the Lord Jesus died, was buried and rose from the dead. Without that, our faith would be empty and there would not be a church (1 Cor. 15:12-14).

d. All that **He is still doing**. Foundational to church life is not only what the Lord Jesus did when He was on Earth, but also what He still is doing today. He has ascended to heaven from where He reigns and still works in the Earth (Rom. 8:34; John 16:23,26-27; 17:20-24; Heb 4:14-15; 7:25; 9:24; 1 John 2:1-2).

e. All that **He still will do**. The Bible declares that the Lord Jesus will come back for a fully restored, glorious and holy Church (Eph. 5:26-27; Acts 3:21; 1 Thess. 5:23). Because of this we can expect the Lord Jesus to continue to build His Church and restore her to her former glory and more. When we keep building what God is building, and build it according to how He wants it built, then success is guaranteed (Ps. 127). The greatest days of the Church are yet to come.

2. **The foundational teachings of Christ.**

Luke 6:47-48 (NKJV) - 47 Whoever comes to Me, and hears My sayings and does them, I will show you whom he is like: 48 He is like a man building a house, who dug deep and laid the foundation on the rock. And when the flood arose, the stream beat vehemently against that house.

Firstly we saw that Jesus is the Rock. Here we read that the foundation is laid on the Rock. In other words, there is another aspect that has to do with the foundation. We can read about this aspect of the foundation in the following passage.

Hebrews 6:1-3 (KJ21) - 1 Therefore, leaving the principles of the doctrine of Christ, let us go on unto perfection, not laying again the foundation of repentance from dead works and of faith toward God, 2 of the doctrine of baptisms and of laying on of hands, and of resurrection of the dead and of eternal judgment. 3 And this we will do, if God permits.

There are seven foundational teachings found in Hebrews 6:1-3. Proverbs 9:1 also says:

Proverbs 9:1 (NKJV) - 1 Wisdom has built her house, she has hewn out her seven pillars.

Let's have a brief look at the seven pillars of the foundation.

a. **Repentance from dead works**

Becoming a Christian is not a case of "just believe". It is repentance and belief (Mark 1:15; Matt. 21:32; Acts 20:21). When people just believe without repenting it leads to hypocrisy. They claim to believe, but do not live accordingly because of lack of repentance.

b. **Faith toward God**

We should not have faith toward ourselves, but faith toward God, toward His Word, toward the Lord Jesus Christ and toward His finished work at the cross. Note that it says faith *toward* God. Toward refers to movement. It is not a dead mental faith that doesn't move people forward in God; it is a faith that moves people towards obedience and towards the purposes of God for their lives (Jam. 2:14-26).

c. **The doctrine of baptisms**

Notice that the word 'baptisms' is plural. The New Testament talks about several baptisms of which the baptism in water and the baptism in the Holy Spirit are the most foundational. Because they are so foundational it is important that these baptisms are being taught and experienced by the people who make up the Church in order for the Church to be strong and secure (Acts 2:38).

d. **The laying on of hands**

The laying on of hands was practiced in the Old Testament as well as in the New Testament for the purpose of impartation and identification. In the New Testament we see it practised in connection with the healing of the sick, with appointing new leaders, with sending people out, with imparting the baptism of the Holy Spirit and imparting the gifts of the Spirit (Acts 5:12; 8:17-19; 19:5-6; 9:41; 13:1-4; 28:8; Mark 16:17; 1 Tim. 4:14; 2 Tim. 1:6). All these things are for strengthening the Church and that is why it is so foundational for building a strong and secure church.

e. **Resurrection of the dead**

This doctrine refers first of all to the resurrection of the Lord Jesus Christ. In his book on Hebrews, Kevin Connor says, "The doctrine of the resurrection of Christ from among the dead is the foundation stone of Christianity". His resurrection was a first fruit (1 Cor. 15:20). His resurrection refers to the resurrection of all men at the end of the age (1 Cor. 15). All men will be raised from the dead and have to give an account for the life they have lived in their bodies (2 Cor. 5:10).

f. **Eternal judgment**

This principle is connected with the resurrection of the dead, because the purpose of the resurrection is so that all men can be judged.

The Lord Jesus was judged for man's sins on the cross and everybody who repents, who places their faith in the finished work of the Lord Jesus on the cross and walks in obedience to the Word of God, will not be judged in the sense of being sent to hell (Rom. 8:1). Only Satan, fallen angels, demons and unrepentant mankind will face this kind of judgement. The believers will be judged according to their works and receive rewards accordingly (1 Cor. 3:10-15; Rom. 2:16; 14:12; 1 John 2:28; 2 Cor. 5:10; Acts 24:25).

The resurrection of the dead and eternal judgement are foundational because they help people to realize that there is an eternity coming. What people do here in this life on Earth will determine where and how they are going to spend eternity. This helps people to put their minds on spiritual and eternal things instead of on natural and temporal things.

g. **Go on unto perfection**

Perfection speaks of being without blemish, of completeness and also of maturity.

All the parts of this aspect of the foundation help us to grow to maturity and to become without blemish. The more mature and perfect the Church becomes - the stronger and more secure she becomes - the more effective she will be in fulfilling her purpose on Earth.

Hebrews 6:3 (KJ21) – [3] And this we will do, if God permits.

In some countries when a person builds his own house and the foundation has been laid, someone from the government comes to check if the foundation is laid correctly before the person is permitted to continue building. When it is laid correctly the government will give a permit to finish the house. If it is not laid correctly, the foundation needs to be repaired before permission is given.

God checks the foundations of the churches we are building, and only gives His permission (blessing) to go on to greater things if the foundations are laid correctly.

A good way of making sure that these foundations are being laid in the life of every church member is by having a membership class which a new candidate has to complete in order to become a member of the church. Good materials to use for this class are *Partnership Guide* by Chip Kawalsingh and *Principles of Church Life* by Bill Scheidler.

3. **The Church in Acts 2.**

Acts 2 is foundational for the Church because in Acts 2 we read about:

- The original outpouring of the Holy Spirit.
- The first sermon that was preached by Peter after the Holy Spirit had been poured out.
- How the original Church functioned and what the principles were that governed it. It is in Acts 2 that we see the blueprint of how any local church should function in order to become strong and secure.

We will find that some of the principles are similar to the ones in Hebrews 6:1-3, whilst others are additional. We will not deal with them extensively; some of the principles will be dealt with more fully in other chapters in this book. Let us look at the major principles on which the early Church was built.

Acts 2:37-47 (NKJV) - 37 Now when they heard this, they were cut to the heart, and said to Peter and the rest of the apostles, "Men and brethren, what shall we do?" 38 Then Peter said to them, "Repent, and let every one of you be baptized in the name of Jesus Christ for the remission of sins; and you shall receive the gift of the Holy Spirit. 39 For the promise is to you and to your children, and to all who are afar off, as many as the Lord our God will call." 40 And with many other words he testified and exhorted them, saying,

"Be saved from this perverse generation." [41] Then those who gladly received his word were baptized; and that day about three thousand souls were added to them. [42] And they continued steadfastly in the apostles' doctrine and fellowship, in the breaking of bread, and in prayers. [43] Then fear came upon every soul, and many wonders and signs were done through the apostles. [44] Now all who believed were together, and had all things in common, [45] and sold their possessions and goods, and divided them among all, as anyone had need. [46] So continuing daily with one accord in the temple, and breaking bread from house to house, they ate their food with gladness and simplicity of heart, [47] praising God and having favour with all the people. And the Lord added to the church daily those who were being saved.

a. **Repentance** - *'Then Peter said to them, "Repent…"'*

The audience that Peter addressed realised that they had sinned against God. Full of remorse they asked Peter, "What shall we do?" Peter answered that first they had to repent. This is similar to the first principle of the foundational doctrine of Christ which we saw in Hebrews 6:1.

Repentance was a foundation stone for the early Church and it should also be for the Church today. It must be laid correctly in the lives of the people who make up the Church in order for the Church to become strong and secure.

b. **Baptism in water** - *'and let every one of you be baptized in the name of Jesus Christ for the remission of sins'*

The second aspect mentioned by Peter was that they had to be baptised in water. Faith is not mentioned here because they had already expressed faith by believing the words of Peter, by asking what they should do with that which Peter had told them.

After people repent and believe, they need to be baptised in water according to the commandment of the Lord Jesus Christ (Matt. 28:19). By obeying the Lord Jesus Christ in baptism people validate their repentance and faith and die to their old sinful life. They bury the old man and are raised up in newness of life (Rom. 6:4; Col. 2:11-15).

c. **Baptism in the Holy Spirit** - *'and you shall receive the gift of the Holy Spirit'*

Repentance, faith and water baptism prepare the way for the Holy Spirit to dwell in the believer and for them to receive the baptism in the Holy Spirit. By receiving the Holy Spirit, and by being baptised in the Holy Spirit, the believer receives power to live in newness of life (the fruits of the Spirit), to speak in tongues and to be used by God in a supernatural way (the gifts of the Spirit) (Rom. 8:9-11; Acts 1:8; 2:1-4; 8:15-21; 19:6; 1 Cor. 12:1-13).

d. **Apostolic teaching** - *'And they continued steadfastly in the apostles' doctrine'*

In order to keep growing, Christians need to keep learning. When they stop learning they stop growing. When they stop growing, they stop changing. When they stop changing, they will not fully become the person God wants them to be (2 Cor. 3:18; Eph. 5:26).

We need to keep a teachable spirit and be willing to be taught by the leaders whom God placed over us for the rest of our lives in order to walk in the fullness of the plan God has for us (Jer. 50:4; Hebr. 13:17).

e. **Fellowship** - *'and fellowship'*

Man was never meant to go through life alone (Gen. 2:18). Christians were never meant to be alone either but to be part of a local church family, where they develop close relationships with other Christians with whom they share their lives. This fulfils a basic need of belonging that every human being has.

In the early Church this close fellowship led to great joy, gladness and great unity amongst each other and an attitude of giving and sharing so that no one was needy:

'Now all who believed were together, and had all things in common, and sold their possessions and goods, and divided them among all, as anyone had need. So continuing daily with one accord in the temple, and breaking bread from house to house, they ate their food with gladness and simplicity of heart,'

In developing fellowship there must be a balance between the corporate church services and the home groups, as the early Church had.

*'So continuing daily with one accord **in the temple (corporate meetings)**, and breaking bread **from house to house' (home group meetings)**.*

Corporate meetings and home group meetings are both important for the Church to become strong and secure. It is in the home group that close relationship can grow and ministries can be developed.

f. **Communion** - *'in the breaking of bread'*

There are several things that the Lord Jesus wants to accomplish through the celebration of communion. Communion should be a time of remembrance and gratefulness for what the Lord has done. It is also a time when we can examine ourselves and commit our lives afresh to the Lord. It is a time when we can receive healing and when unity with the other members of the church is confirmed and strengthened (1 Cor. 11:24-25; 28). It is through the elements of the bread and the wine, which represent the body and the blood of the Lord Jesus Christ that the Lord Jesus wants to touch us, strengthen us, unite us, fill us, heal us and impart life to us.

All these things are for the strengthening of the Church and that is why they are foundational for the building of strong and secure churches.

g. **Prayer** - *'and in prayers'*

It is through prayer that we connect ourselves with God and strengthen and cultivate our relationship with Him. It is through prayer that God's will is fulfilled in our lives, churches, communities, nations, continents, and the whole Earth (Matt. 6:10; 1 John 5:14). Prayer is a powerful weapon and it should not be neglected by the believer individually or the Church corporately. The Church should be a house of prayer (Matt. 21:13).

h. **Fear of God** - *'Then fear came upon every soul'*

The fear of God protects us from allowing compromise to come into our lives and churches, because we know that in the end we will suffer the consequences. The fear of God helps us to walk and to grow in holiness and this causes the Church to become strong and secure (Acts 9:31).

i. **Signs and wonders** - *'and many wonders and signs were done through the apostles'*

The Lord Jesus is alive and sitting at the right-hand of God from where He is still working in the Earth by the Holy Spirit though the Church (Acts 4:30; 5:12; 6:8; 14:3). Signs and wonders did not stop when the first apostles died.

Signs and wonders are not an end in themselves, but a means to an end. The purpose of signs and wonders is that souls continue to be saved and enter into a lasting relationship with the Lord Jesus Christ (John 5:14). They are given for the growth and strengthening of the Church (1 Cor. 12:7; 14:3).

j. **Praise and worship** - *'praising God'*

As the Church is the house of God, God's presence is one of the most important elements of church life (Ps. 16:11). God wants to be in the midst of His people (Ex. 25:8; Eph. 2:19-22; Matt. 18:20). God's presence is attracted by people who worship Him in spirit and truth (John 4:23-24). God dwells in the midst of the praises of His people (Ps. 22:3), and where God is there is blessing (2 Sam. 6:12) and the favour of God without which the Church cannot be built (Ps. 127).

k. **Favour** - *'having favour with all the people'*

The impact the gospel had on people caused them to have favour with men.

When the world sees integrity in our conduct, and when they see that we really care because we are willing to play a role in taking care of the needs of people in our communities, it will honour the name of the Lord Jesus and it will bring the favour of the people (Dan. 1:9; Gen. 39:21; Jam. 1:27).

I. **Church membership** - *'And the Lord added to the church daily those who were being saved.'*

The pattern we see in the book of Acts is that people first were added to the Lord.

> **Acts 5:14 (NKJV) - 14 'And believers were increasingly added to the Lord, multitudes of both men and women,'**

> **Acts 11:24 (NKJV) 24 'For he was a good man, full of the Holy Spirit and of faith. And a great many people were added to the Lord.'**

When people become born again they are born into the Kingdom of God (John 3:3-5). They are added to the Lord and they become part of the universal Church; but the pattern we see in the book of Acts is that after people were added to the Lord they were added to a local church as well.

> **Acts 2:41 (NKJV) - 41 'Then those who gladly received his word were baptized; and that day about three thousand souls were added to them.'**

Every believer should be added to a specific local church and commit themselves to local church life based on the principles which we have seen in Acts 2.

There are Christians who feel threatened by church membership, either because they have been hurt in the past or because they want to have freedom and do not want to be accountable to human authority. They often excuse themselves by saying that they are already part of the universal Church.

By the spiritual birth someone becomes part of the universal Church, just as every human being becomes part of the human race by the natural birth. But Christians who fail to commit themselves to the life of a local church become spiritual orphans. They are without a specific spiritual family and without a specific spiritual home. Because of this they miss out on:

- Relationships (Col. 2:2).
- Sense of belonging (1 Cor. 12:12-27).
- Spiritual growth (Ps. 92:13; 1 Thess. 5:12; Eph. 4:11-16).
- Protection (1 Cor. 11:1-10; Ps. 91).
- Sense of value by using their talents and gifts (Rom. 12:3-8; 1 Cor. 12:18).

In other words, they are missing out on all that will cause them to become a strong and stable Christian who will take their God-given place in the Kingdom of God.

Strong and Secure Churches and Church Growth

'And the Lord added to the church daily those who were being saved.'

Pastors often look for keys to unlock growth in their churches. In their search for church growth they often chase all kinds of new moves and try all kinds of new methods, hoping that one of them will cause their churches to grow. Brother Dick Iverson has said that this is like chasing the golden pot at the end of the rainbow. Every time you get there it is gone. Brother Iverson said, "The greatest key to church growth is to make the basics beautiful". When the members of the church become excited for basic things like prayer, fellowship, worship and evangelism the church will grow.

The reason that the early Church grew so rapidly was that it was built on all of these basic principles. That is why a wise builder makes sure that the foundation is laid well, not according to the latest trend but according to the pattern God has laid down for us in His Word. That will unlock church growth and we will see addition coming to our churches also.

Strong and Secure Churches and Leadership Development

In the development of strong and secure churches leadership is crucial. Everything stands and falls with leadership, it is needed in all kinds of areas and levels in church life. Leadership is needed in the eldership, children's work, house groups and youth to mention just a few.

When a church is in a pioneering stage, the ones who pioneer do most of the work themselves. But as the church grows other leaders are needed to carry part of the burden in order for the church to continue to develop and for the Pastor not to get burned out (Ex. 18:13-27; Acts 6:1-7). This also unlocks the potential that the other leaders have and it will make the church more capable and effective in fulfilling her purpose.

When appointing new leaders it is very important that the person who is placed in leadership is someone with the right character, the right capabilities and the same spirit as the Pastor of the church (Phil. 2:20; 1 Tim. 3:1-13; Tit. 1:5-9. 1 Chron. 12:16-21; Judges 7:18).

People do not usually have these three qualities automatically; they need to be developed. As the Lord Jesus developed 12 disciples into apostles who carried the vision of the Lord Jesus Christ, leaders in our churches should also be developed to carry the heart of the Pastor, and work to fulfil the vision the Pastor has for the house. This will cause the church to be one in spirit and purpose so that nothing will be impossible to achieve (Ps. 133; Phil. 2; Rom. 15:5; 2 Cor. 13:11).

> Genesis 11:6 - 6 ' And the LORD said, "Indeed the people are one and they all have one language, and this is what they begin to do; now nothing that they propose to do will be withheld from them.'

Every development starts with teaching (Rom. 10:17). A good book for training leaders is *Formation Leadership* by Chip Kawalsingh.

CONCLUSION

Everything that man originates is temporal, but the Church is going to last forever because God is the One who originated it. The Church is God's plan and it will last forever. When Christians get a vision for the Church and commit themselves to it, co-operate with God's plan and invest their lives in something that has eternal value, then they will produce lasting fruit. This will result in a fulfilled Christian life with the satisfaction of seeing the production of fruit that lasts and makes a difference for eternity.

BUILDING WITH A BIBLICAL FRAMEWORK

INTRODUCTION

In charismatic circles, it is not always common to speak about structure. The idea is sometimes held that structure is tantamount to lack of freedom for the Holy Spirit. There is a conception that "structure" is always opposite to "life". When we see it like this, talking about structure and framework doesn't seem to be beneficial to the development of growing, healthy churches. But the question is: "Is this true?" If not, why is a Biblical framework important for a healthy, growing church and what is a Biblical structure?

WHY A FRAMEWORK?

When we look at creation, we see that all the living things that God has created have structure. In creation, we also see that structure is not opposed to life, but it is meant to support and uphold life. Look, for example, at the ribs or veins of a leaf. They support and uphold the living cells, so that the leaf can function how God designed it and meant it to be. Another example is that of the human body. Can you imagine how your body would function without your skeleton? The Church is likened to a body.

1 Corinthians 12:27 (NKJV) - 27 Now you are the body of Christ, and members individually.

As the natural body cannot function without a structure, so a church cannot function and be successful without a Biblical framework.

Structure only becomes a hindrance to growth and development, when it doesn't grow and develop when the cells multiply and the organism grows. But this doesn't mean that structure is not needed.

STRONG AND SAFE HOUSES NEED GOOD FRAMEWORKS

Let us consider the analogy of a house. We know that a house needs a good foundation that can withstand the test of the floods. It also needs a good structure that can stand the test of the storms.

Take for example, the tabernacle of Moses, which was the house of God from the time of Moses to the time of King David in the Old Testament. The foundation of the tabernacle was made of silver sockets (Ex. 25:19, 21, 25, 32, 37; Ex. 27:10-12, 14-18). Wooden boards were placed in these sockets and these boards together formed the structure of the tabernacle. The structure upheld the curtains and the coverings, so that inside the tabernacle, all that God had ordained could be carried out, in order for God to live in the midst of them (Ex. 25:8; Ex. 26:31-32; Ex. 27). When the desert storms came, the tabernacle didn't collapse, but it stood strong because of the solid structure.

As the house of God in the Old Testament needed a good framework, so does the house of God in the New Testament, that is, the Church (1 Tim. 3:15).

THE NEED FOR GOVERNMENT

Government is the key word when we talk about a structure. Chapter eight of this book will deal with this subject in more detail. It is in this chapter that we are going to look at the subject in a more general sense.

Without government, things lead to chaos. Take for example, the Universe. It is governed by laws such as the law of gravity. These laws cause the universe and things on earth to function in an orderly way. Without these laws there would be disorder, and life could not exist and function.

Another example is that of the family. In a family there is a need for parents that bring order so that the family can function in happiness and harmony. The same is true for society:

Romans 13:1-2 (NIV) - [1] Everyone must submit himself to the governing authorities, for there is no authority except that which God has established. The authorities that exist have been established by God. [2] Consequently, he who rebels against the authority is rebelling against what God has instituted, and those who do so will bring judgment on themselves.

Can you imagine if there was no government leading the country? If there were no laws that the citizens had to live by? It would be impossible to live a happy life in that country. Without government there is no order, no direction and therefore no peace and harmony.

1 Timothy 2:1-2 (New King James Version) - [1] Therefore I exhort first of all that supplications, prayers, intercessions, and giving of thanks be made for all men, [2] for kings and all who are in authority, that we may lead a quiet and peaceable life in all godliness and reverence.

As there is a need for government in the universe, in the family and in society, there is also a need for government in the Church. The question is no longer *if* government is needed in the Church. The question is what kind of government does God have for His Church? How is this government structured?

Church Government

Western Christians are so used to living in countries that are being governed in a democratic way, that they may think that the Kingdom of God is also governed in the same way. But it is there where things often go wrong. The Kingdom of God is not a democracy. In the Kingdom of God, we are under the rule of God, which is called a theocracy. God is all-knowing and He knows what is best. In the Kingdom of God, God's will is law whether we like His will or not. The only option we have is to submit to His will and obey it. This may sound scary to some, but we must realise that God is a good and loving God, and we can trust that His will is ultimately for our best interests.

What about the Church? How should the Church be governed? The Church, as part of the Kingdom of God, is ruled by the same principles that govern the Kingdom. We saw that the Kingdom of God is not ruled in a democratic way and that is why the Church, as part of the Kingdom of God, should not be governed in a democratic way. We saw that the Kingdom of God is a theocracy, therefore the Church, as part of the Kingdom of God, is also ruled in a theocratic manner. The Church is not ruled by the people, but by God. The Lord Jesus is the head of the Church.

Colossians 1:18 (NIV) - [18] And He is the head of the body, the church; He is the beginning and the firstborn from among the dead, so that in everything He might have the supremacy.

The way God rules in the Church is through people whom He calls and equips to govern and lead the Church (Eph. 4:11). God invests in them and delegates a measure of authority as He wills and to whom He wills. The leadership have the responsibility to lead the Church in a way that reflects the nature and character of Christ. They are Christ's representatives and therefore must lead in a Christ-like manner (Phil. 2:5-8; 1 Pet. 5:1-4; Matt. 23:11).

TEAM OF ELDERS

When we look at how the leadership of the Church was structured in the Bible, we can see that local churches were led by a group of people called "elders".

Acts 14:23 (NIV) - [23] Paul and Barnabas appointed elders for them in each church and, with prayer and fasting, committed them to the Lord, in whom they had put their trust.

Every time when the Bible speaks about the leadership of the Church, it speaks about it in the plural.

Hebrews 13:7 (NIV) - [7] Remember your leaders, who spoke the word of God to you. Consider the outcome of their way of life and imitate their faith.

Hebrews 13:17 (NIV) - [17] Obey your leaders and submit to their authority. They keep watch over you as men who must give an account. Obey them so that their work will be a joy, not a burden, for that would be of no advantage to you.

Hebrews 13:24 (NIV) - [24] Greet all your leaders and all God's people. Those from Italy send you their greetings.

Read also Acts 15:2; 16:4; 20:17; 21:17-18; 1 Tim. 5:17-21; Tit. 1:5; Jam. 5:14; 1 Pet. 5:1; Rev. 4:4.

When we read all these Scriptures, we can conclude that the way God wants His Church to be led is by a team of leaders called elders. It is not a one-man show.

A remark: When a church is in its pioneering stage and no other fit leaders are available, then there can be a period when one person is leading the church. This is acceptable for the stage the church is in at that moment. But as the church develops, a team of leaders should be developed.

PLURALITY AND ORDER

The way that the leadership is structured in the Church is a reflection of who God is and how He governs.

When we look at God, we see that He is plural, that is He is Father, Son and Holy Spirit, and yet one (1 John 5:7). So God is a team of three persons and one at the same time. As God is a team, so the leadership of the church should be a team.

There are many benefits to leading the church as a team. Here are some:

1. No one man has all the giftings that are needed to lead the church. Other team members provide additional strengths to the team and additional input to the church.
2. A team gives the opportunity for sharing the burden of the ministry so that one man will not experience a burn out.
3. A team provides checks and balances for all the members of the team.

Although there is plurality in the Godhead, there is also order. Bill Scheidler, in his book *The Keys to Healthy Growing Churches*, says that in the Godhead "there is equality of persons (Phil. 2:6), and yet there is at the same time an order of headship (1 Cor. 11:3)". The Father sent the Son, and the Son sent the Holy Spirit. The Spirit bears witness to the Son, and the Son bears witness to the Father. The Father becomes the ultimate figure in the Godhead (1 Cor. 15:27)".

The same is true for the team of leaders of the church. Without an understanding of order in the team and an understanding of what each one's role of responsibility is, the team can be divided over all kinds of issues and therefore be hindered in fulfilling their God-given mission. Especially in the western world, people feel entitled to have their own opinion and they are willing to fight for their opinion even at the cost of division. This is often so because there is no understanding of authority. Chip Kawalsingh, in his book *Formation Leadership*, says, "opinion without a revelation of authority leads to division". A divided church will not progress and last (Mark 3:25-26).

Again, for the church to be united and progressing there has to be the same type of leadership model that there is in the Godhead. As the Father is the ultimate figure in the Godhead, so in the team of elders there is one who is the leader of the team. He is the one that God has appointed and anointed to lead the team and the church in their God-given destiny. Although there is equality as persons, there is a difference of function. This should be seen and respected.

The leader of the eldership team is also called the set-man. He is the visionary. The vision of the set-man is the vision that should be pursued. When this is done, there will be great unity and nothing will be impossible for that church. Take, for example, the story of Gideon defeating the Midianite army with 300 men. Look at what it says:

> Judges 7 (NIV) - [17] "Watch me," he told them. "Follow my lead. When I get to the edge of the camp, do exactly as I do. [18] When I and all who are with me blow our trumpets, then from all around the camp blow yours and shout, 'For the LORD and for Gideon.' "

God spoke to Gideon to conquer the vast army of the Midianites with only 300 men. Although, humanly speaking, they could never have conquered an army that was so much larger than the 300 men they had, they still did it because they embraced the vision that God gave to Gideon and were willing to run with that vision. As a result they experienced breakthrough and advancement.

We saw that God structured the leadership of the Church in such a way that there is, on the one hand, plurality of leadership and on the other hand a team leader, a set-man. Throughout the whole Bible we can see this functioning. We read about:

1. Old Testament:
    a. Moses and the elders (Num. 11:16, 24, 30; Deut. 27:1 etc).
    b. Joshua and the elders (Josh. 7:6; 8:10; 23:2; 24:1, 31; Jud. 2:7).
    c. David and the elders (1 Chron. 15:25; 21:16).

2. New Testament:
    a. James and the elders (Acts 21:18).
    b. Timothy and the elders (1 Tim. 3).
    c. Titus and the elders (Tit. 1:5-9).
    d. The Lamb and the twenty-four elders (Rev. 4:2-4; 5:6 etc).

QUALIFICATIONS FOR ELDERS

The Bible is also clear that elders have to have certain qualifications. Not just anybody can function as an elder. The qualifications are listed in Timothy 3:1-7 and Titus 1:5-9. Bill Scheidler in his book *The Keys to Healthy Growing Churches* says that you can group the qualifications of potential elders in four categories:

1. Proven character.
2. Spiritual vision. That is to see clearly God's purposes and to have the maturity to bring the sacrifices to see those purposes come to pass.
3. Orderly homes.
4. Spiritual gifting.

SUPPORT LEADERS

As the church grows and develops, there will also be a need for support leaders that will take up responsibilities in the church as they are delegated to them from the eldership of the church. This is necessary to fulfil the growing needs that the church will have as it multiplies. This was also the case in the early Church.

Acts 6 (NKJV) - [1] Now in those days, when the number of the disciples was multiplying, there arose a complaint against the Hebrews by the Hellenists, because their widows were neglected in the daily distribution. [2] Then the twelve summoned the multitude of the disciples and said, "It is not desirable that we should leave the word of God and serve tables. [3] Therefore, brethren, seek out from among you seven men of good reputation, full of the Holy Spirit and wisdom, whom we may appoint over this business; [4] but we will give ourselves continually to prayer and to the ministry of the word." [5] And the saying pleased the whole multitude. And they chose Stephen, a man full of faith and the Holy Spirit, and Philip, Prochorus, Nicanor, Timon, Parmenas, and Nicolas, a proselyte from Antioch, [6] whom they set before the apostles; and when they had prayed, they laid hands on them. [7] Then the word of God spread, and the number of the disciples multiplied greatly in Jerusalem, and a great many of the priests were obedient to the faith.

When we read these verses we can see the need for support leaders. At first the apostles did all the work themselves but, as the Church grew, the work became too much. So they changed the structure, that is, the way the Church was led, in order for the Church to continue to grow.

We have already seen in this chapter that in nature structure only becomes a hindrance to growth and development when it doesn't grow and develop with the development of the organism. The Church is like an organism in the sense that when it is alive it grows. When it grows its structure should also grow and change with it.

The way a group of 50 people can be led is different to how 1,000 should be led. The eldership would be wise to change the structure when the growth of the church demands it, in order for the church to continue to grow. They do this by delegating part of their authority to others, so that they can lead a particular part of the church and cause it to develop even further. The result is that there will be room for more growth.

Acts 6 (NKJV) - 7 Then the word of God spread, and the number of the disciples multiplied greatly in Jerusalem, and a great many of the priests were obedient to the faith.

The word "then" refers to what has happened in the Scriptures before verse 7. In verses 1-6 we read that the apostles appointed support leaders. As a result of this, the word of God spread even further and the disciples multiplied greatly.

QUALIFICATIONS OF A SUPPORT LEADER

In the appointing of support leaders in Acts 6, we see also that support leaders weren't just anybody. It is not just appointing people into leadership, but appointing the right kind of people. It is very important that the person who is placed in leadership is someone with the right qualifications.

From Acts 6:1-6 we can detect some of the qualifications that were necessary before appointing support leaders.

1. Men of good reputation.
2. Full of the Holy Spirit.
3. Full of wisdom.
4. Full of faith.

Moses also appointed support leaders.

Exodus 18:21 (NKJV) - 21 Moreover you shall select from all the people able men, such as fear God, men of truth, hating covetousness; and place such over them to be rulers of thousands, rulers of hundreds, rulers of fifties, and rulers of tens.

In this Scripture we can see some more qualifications that are required from support leaders.

1. Able men.
2. Who fear God.
3. Men of truth.
4. Hating covetousness.

UNITY

Besides the qualifications that are mentioned above, it is important that all the support leaders in the church are willing to flow together in unity. This can only happen when all the support leaders pursue one and the same vision. The gifting that everybody has will differ, personalities will differ, but the vision that they need to pursue needs to be the same - that is the vision of the set-man that God has placed in that house. They need to become of one and the same spirit as the Pastor of the church so that they all flow in unity with each other (Phil. 2:20; 1 Tim. 3:1-13; Titus 1:5-9; 1 Chron. 12:16-21; Judges 7:18).

We can see an example of this in the life of Moses when 70 elders were appointed.

Numbers 1:16-17; 24-25 (NKJV) - [16] So the LORD said to Moses: "Gather to Me seventy men of the elders of Israel, whom you know to be the elders of the people and officers over them; bring them to the tabernacle of meeting, that they may stand there with you. [17] Then I will come down and talk with you there. I will take of the Spirit that is upon you and will put the same upon them; and they shall bear the burden of the people with you, that you may not bear it yourself alone.

[24] So Moses went out and told the people the words of the LORD, and he gathered the seventy men of the elders of the people and placed them around the tabernacle. [25] Then the LORD came down in the cloud, and spoke to him, and took of the Spirit that was upon him, and placed the same upon the seventy elders; and it happened, when the Spirit rested upon them, that they prophesied, although they never did so again.

When the set-man, the elders and the support leaders all flow in unity, it attracts the blessings of God and all things become possible.

Psalm 133:1, 3 (NKJV) - [1] Behold, how good and how pleasant it is for brethren to dwell together in unity! ... [3] ... For there the LORD commanded the blessing — Life forevermore.

Genesis 11:6 (NKJV) - 6 And the LORD said, "Indeed the people are one and they all have one language, and this is what they begin to do; now nothing that they propose to do will be withheld from them.

The Lord Jesus has said:

Matthew 18:19 (NKJV) - 19 "Again I say to you that if two of you agree on earth concerning anything that they ask, it will be done for them by My Father in heaven."

CONCLUSION

Structure holds things together and enables a group of people, who are different from each other in many ways, to flow together in unity so they can function together and grow as they were intended. When structure is used correctly and wisely it will cause great harmony and unity in the church, and unity will attract the presence of God and with it God's blessings. So instead of structure diminishing the flow of the Spirit and the blessing of God, it will cause God's Spirit to move mightily and the church can exist and grow as God intends it to.

Chapter 4 — Gordon Tose

The Importance of the Local Church

It is undoubtedly true that the local church, when it functions as it should, is the main vehicle by which the Kingdom of God is both established and extended. This is because it is in the local church that people can learn to be effective in their Christian walk.

In the book of Ephesians the apostle Paul uses various names and imagery to describe and to emphasise different aspects of the Church. In chapter 1:23 the Church is referred to as "His body" or "the Body of Christ". In chapter 2:21 the image is that of the Temple of God. In chapter 3:15 the Church becomes the Family of God, while in chapter 5:32 the image is that of a bride and so the Church becomes the Bride of Christ. Finally, for the purpose of this study, the Church in chapter 6:10-17 becomes the Army of God. Paul is actually using these terms in the context of the universal Church but they will never be a reality in the universal Church unless they are first demonstrated within the framework of the local church.

The Body of Christ

Ephesians 1:22-23 (NIV) - "And God placed all things under his feet and appointed him to be the head over everything for the church, which is his body, the fullness of him who fills everything in every way"

Ephesians 4:16 (NIV) - "From him the whole body, joined and held together by every supporting ligament, grows and builds itself up in love, as each part does its work."

When comparing the Church to the human body, the obvious scripture to refer to is 1 Corinthians 12. In this portion of scripture we see that for the human body to function as it was designed to, all the individual parts have to function properly. This is true also of the Church. This scripture also tells us that the individual parts of our body function differently and that all these different functions are necessary. Again this is also true of the Church. Having said that, it appears to be human nature to place a higher value on some functions, or gifts, than on others. Thankfully the distribution of these gifts is the responsibility of the Lord and not ourselves.

1 Corinthians 12:11 - (NIV) "All these (gifts) are the work of the same Spirit and he gives them to each one just as he determines."

For example, someone can want to be a preacher as much as they like, but they either have the gift or they don't. Certainly it is our responsibility as individuals to develop the gift within us, but we cannot manufacture the gift. In fact, continuing with the example of preaching, if God brought together dozens of preachers within the confines of one local church, then you would have to wonder at the wisdom of that, as the opportunity for everyone to exercise their gift would be limited. What the Church does need, and what God will supply, are many people gifted as servers, givers and helpers, because in any church there are many opportunities for those kinds of ministries to flourish. As leaders, it is our responsibility to create an environment in which the congregation can identify and be released in the gifts that they have.

Ephesians 4:11-12 (NIV) - "It was he (Jesus) who gave some to be apostles, some to be prophets, some to be evangelists, and some to be pastors and teachers, to prepare God's people for works of service so that the body of Christ may be built up."

What is frustrating and wasteful, for both the individual concerned and the church as a whole, is when somebody tries to operate outside their gifting. Using a football analogy, if I am really a centre back but am trying to operate as a striker, I am not going to be fulfilled. I may well be a good footballer but operating out of position isn't going to bless anybody. It's not going to bless me and it's not going to bless the team. When we all begin functioning as we should, not waiting to be asked, not wanting to be given a title, then the result is that everybody's needs are met, whether those needs be spiritual, emotional or practical. It's as those needs are met that the Kingdom of God in a given locality is established and then extended as it becomes increasingly attractive to the world outside.

THE TEMPLE OF GOD

Ephesians 2:19-22 (NIV) - "Consequently, you are no longer foreigners and aliens, but fellow citizens with God's people and members of God's household, built on the foundation of the apostles and prophets, with Christ Jesus himself as the chief cornerstone. In him the whole building is joined together and rises to become a holy temple in the Lord. And in him you too are being built together to become a dwelling in which God lives by his Spirit."

1 Corinthians 3:16 (NIV) - "Don't you know that you yourselves are God's temple and that God's Spirit lives in you?"

1 Corinthians 6:19 (NIV) - "Do you not know that your body is a temple of the Holy Spirit?"

One secular definition of a temple is "a building devoted to the worship of, or regarded as the dwelling place of a god or gods." From that we can see that a temple should be a place where there is the manifested presence of God or, to put it another way, if God dwells in the temple we should be able to detect His presence. Taking that a step further, for us individually to be a Temple of God, our lives should demonstrate God's presence. For that to happen our lives should display certain qualities, the same qualities or characteristics that you would find in a temple.

Firstly we need to be a worshipper. Let's not forget that a temple is "a building devoted to worship." John 4:24, talks of worshipping God "in spirit and in truth." Worshipping "in truth" involves the physical demonstration of worship e.g. singing, raising our hands etc. Worshipping "in spirit" is to worship wholeheartedly. Worshipping "in truth" doesn't automatically mean that we are worshipping "in spirit", but when we worship "in spirit" we will automatically worship "in truth." Worshipping "in spirit" is a choice based not on our present circumstances but on how much we have to thank God for. There are times when we feel overwhelmed by our present circumstances and worshipping God becomes difficult which is where our involvement in a local church is of utmost importance. There is a phrase, commonly used, that goes "God inhabits the praises of His people." This is based on Psalm 22:3 (King James Version). One example of how this works is that we can be in a spiritually dry place and yet because of the praise and worship being offered up by everybody else we are motivated to drag ourselves out of our preoccupation and as God ministers to His people, we too can receive a touch from God that otherwise we may have missed.

Secondly we need to be holy, for surely a temple is a holy place: indeed God expects us to be holy.

1 Peter 1:16 (NIV) - "Be holy, because I am holy."

Hebrews 12:14 (NIV) - "Make every effort to live in peace with all men and to be holy; without holiness no one will see the Lord."

The problem with holiness is that it's a quality that does not come to us easily. My experience is that we are more likely to be holy if we are rooted in a local church. It is undoubtedly true that as Christians we are able to resist temptation (see 1 Corinthians 10:13). It is also true that we have at least an intellectual understanding that nothing escapes God's attention. Yet neither of these seems to prevent us from giving in to temptation. An involvement in church entails a degree of accountability. In other words, the people we mix with aren't impressed by our reasons for failure. Isolated Christians are vulnerable. Yes they have God's Word, but what they don't have is the benefit of seeing the Word being worked out in the lives of others. Nor do they have the encouragement of others, and of course that encouragement can include discipline. Without example and encouragement it is a lot easier to fall and a lot more difficult to get back up.

The third function of a temple is that it's a place where sacrifices are offered. The prescribed forms of sacrifice in the New Testament are things like our praise, our time, our abilities and our money. If you think about all these different expressions of sacrificial giving, they are more or less centred on the local church. If we are not part of a church, just how much of what we have to sacrifice would we actually give as an offering to God?

THE FAMILY OF GOD AND THE BRIDE OF CHRIST

Ephesians 2:19 - (NIV) "Consequently, you are no longer foreigners and aliens, but fellow citizens with God's people and members of God's household (or members of God's family)."

Ephesians 3:14-15 (NIV) "For this reason I kneel before the Father, from whom his whole family in heaven and on earth derives its name."

Ephesians 5:31-32 (NIV) - "For this reason a man will leave his father and mother and be united to his wife, and the two will become one flesh." This is a profound mystery—but I am talking about Christ and the church."

The main thrust of both these aspects of the church is relationships, which, potentially, is a subject of some complexity because it revolves around people. There are three scriptures concerning relationships that really get to the heart of the matter.

John 17:20, 23 (NIV) - "My prayer is not for them alone (the disciples). I pray also for those who will believe in me through their message (that's you and me)... May they be brought to complete unity to let the world know that you sent me and have loved them even as you have loved me."

Psalm 133:1, 3 (KJV) - "Behold how good and how pleasant it is for brethren to dwell together in unity! ... For there the LORD commanded his blessing."

Ephesians 4:1-3 (NIV) - "As a prisoner for the Lord, then, I urge you to live a life worthy of the calling you have received. Be completely humble and gentle; be patient, bearing with one another in love. Make every effort to keep the unity of the Spirit through the bond of peace."

From these three scriptures we see firstly that the state of our relationships is at the very heart of Jesus as this is what preoccupied Him as he faced the prospect of crucifixion. Secondly we see that good relationships between people, over the long term, cannot be taken for granted. If it was natural for us to remain in a state of relational harmony with each other, why would Jesus feel the need to pray for it? In fact it is so unnatural that where good relationships exist, Jesus says, they point to God. Thirdly we note that a consequence of good relationships is the blessing of God, the reason for that being that maintaining them is often blood, sweat and tears. It is my belief that these three scriptures apply to all our relationships, be they with our natural family or otherwise.

It is the experience of many that when relationships become seriously strained, what often happens is that there is a continuation of relationships with our blood relatives, whereas non blood relationships often break down. This is a consequence of the fact that our parents will always be our parents no matter how controlling and manipulative some can be, and our children will always be our children irrespective of how much grief they sometimes put us through. To God, these blood ties are no more important than our other relationships despite the often-used expression "Blood is thicker than water" which implies that blood relationships are the strongest relationships we have. This viewpoint is put in doubt by the following scriptures from Proverbs.

Proverbs 17:17 (Amplified) - "A friend loves at all times, and is born, as is a brother, for adversity."

Proverbs 18:24 (NIV) - "A man of many companions may come to ruin, but there is a friend who sticks closer than a brother."

Proverbs 27:10 (Amplified) - "Your own friend and your father's friend, forsake them not, neither go to your brother's house in the day of your calamity. Better is a neighbour who is near in spirit than a brother who is far off in heart."

This is not to say that our other relationships are more fulfilling than our natural family relationships. What is undoubtedly true is that each relationship we have should be judged on its merits and not on the basis of whether or not there is a blood tie. Speaking for myself the person I love most in my life, the one I would most willingly sacrifice myself for, is my wife. My wife is obviously not a blood tie. King David's deepest, dearest and most meaningful relationship was with his friend Jonathan. Blood automatically being thicker than water is simply not true.

Referring back to Ephesians 5:31-32 and the image of the Church being the Bride of Christ, the "mystery" is not that the relationship between Christ and the Church is a reflection of marriage, but that the natural relationship of marriage is supposed to reflect Christ's spiritual relationship with the Church. Surely the same can be said of all our relationships, that they too should be based on the same principles as that which Jesus demonstrates in His relationship with us - that principle being love. Jesus himself said in John 15:13 (NIV) *"Greater love has no one than this, that he lay down his life for his friends."* Isn't that what Jesus did for us? A brilliant picture of Jesus' love for us is presented in John 13 when He washes the feet of His disciples. What makes this brilliant is when we realise just whose feet He washed. He washed the feet of Thomas who would doubt Him, the feet of Peter who would disown Him, even the feet of Judas who would betray Him. Of course, as Jesus does for us so we are to do for others and as Jesus loves us we are to love others.

John 13:14-15 (NIV) - "Now that I, your Lord and Teacher, have washed your feet, you also should wash one another's feet. I have set you an example that you should do as I have done for you."

If we love someone then there is obviously a desire to have fellowship with them and to spend time with them. A love for our fellow brothers and sisters in Christ is demonstrated by us desiring to spend time together and this is best achieved by embracing the reality of the local church as the focal point of our relationships.

Of course, love is also demonstrated by the giving of support. There are times when, without the support of others, our relationship with God would not be as it should be. I'm reminded of the account in Luke 5 when Jesus healed the paralytic who by his own efforts couldn't reach Jesus. He needed his friends to carry him to the roof, to dig through the roof and to lower him from the roof right in front of Jesus. Likewise, spiritually speaking, we sometimes need our friends to put us back in touch with Jesus. It's in the local church where we receive the benefits of faithfulness and forgiveness from others who are motivated by Jesus' faithfulness and forgiveness towards them. In addition, it's in the local church where the Word of God is preached and where we're ministered to as we worship. It's the local church that is a source of Godly direction and encouragement which enables us to overcome our three enemies - the devil, the influence of the world and our own carnal nature. As Christ's Bride, according to the Word, we are supposed to be "without stain, wrinkle or any other blemish, but holy and blameless." We have more chance of being that if we are an integral part of a group.

It would be reasonable to state that the local church, as the Family of God, places people in a community that is committed to each other and that is motivated by love for each other. As the Bride of Christ, the local church enables people to rightly relate to God. These relational benefits of the church help us therefore to fulfil the two greatest commandments of loving God and loving our neighbour as ourselves.

The Army of God

Ephesians 6:10-17 (NIV) - "Finally, be strong in the Lord and in his mighty power. Put on the full armour of God so that you can take your stand against the devil's schemes. For our struggle is not against flesh and blood, but against the rulers, against the authorities, against the powers of this dark world and against the spiritual forces of evil in the heavenly realms. Therefore put on the full armour of God, so that when the day of evil comes, you may be able to stand your ground, and after you have done everything, to stand. Stand firm then, with the belt of truth buckled around your waist, with the breastplate of righteousness in place, and with your feet fitted with the readiness that comes from the gospel of peace. In addition to all this, take up the shield of faith, with which you can extinguish all the flaming arrows of the evil one. Take the helmet of salvation and the sword of the Spirit, which is the word of God."

So, whilst the phrase "the army of God" isn't actually used, the imagery certainly points to that particular function. What that makes us therefore is soldiers.

2 Timothy 2:3 (NIV) - "Endure hardship with us like a good soldier of Christ Jesus."

What soldiers are trained to do is fight and likewise, as soldiers, this is what we are called to do although the weapons we fight with are not the kind of weapons the world would recognise as such.

2 Corinthians 10:3-4 (NIV) - "For though we live in the world, we do not wage war as the world does. The weapons we fight with are not the weapons of the world. On the contrary, they have divine power to demolish strongholds."

What may encourage us is that as "a good soldier of Jesus Christ," at least we are on the winning side. What is less encouraging is the undoubted fact that in any war, even on the winning side, there are always casualties, which is why Paul warns us in 1 Corinthians 10:12 (NIV) *"So, if you think you are standing firm, be careful you do not fall."* The way to avoid falling is to wear *"the full amour of God".*

The "helmet of salvation" is without doubt the foundational garment because, first and foremost, we have to accept that we are saved. We do this by faith which is why the "helmet of salvation" and the "shield of faith" are linked. Our salvation gives us the right to become "a child of God" (see John 1:12-13) and as such we are assured of our Father's love. This is true even during those times when our lives are not very glorifying to God. A casual look at the life of Kind David confirms this point of view. Some Christians, because of certain issues in their lives, have surrendered the peace and the joy that their salvation should bring. Whilst it may be imperative that these issues are dealt with, let us not fall into the trap of doubting our salvation, or believing that we somehow have to earn it, or lacking the faith to believe that, whatever the circumstances of our life, God is with us.

The "belt of truth" and the "breastplate of righteousness" are not so much about our beliefs but our actions. The "belt of truth" speaks of integrity. Integrity for the Christian means being a person of *the* Word, not just a person of our word. The "breastplate of righteousness" speaks of being in right standing before God. It is impossible to be in right standing before God if our lives lack integrity and in this way the belt and the breastplate are linked. This link however, is even more far reaching because if, through lack of integrity, we feel we are not in the place we should be with God, then this can even lead to a doubting of our salvation. A lack of integrity also adversely affects our testimony which renders ineffective "our feet fitted with the readiness that comes from the gospel of peace."

The last piece of armour is the "sword of the Spirit which is the word of God." If we base our lives on God's Word then we will undoubtedly be successful. Basing our marriages and our other relationships on God's Word will ensure we will be successful relationally. Basing the handling of our finances on God's Word ensures we will be prosperous; bearing in mind that prosperity is having more than enough. Basing our very life on God's Word ensures peace and joy irrespective of our circumstances. Success generally does not go unnoticed and people will see our success which then gives us the opportunity of presenting to them the good news of the gospel and makes our testimony all the more powerful because people can see the truth of it.

It is a fact that the degree of success in our lives is linked to the degree of our imperfection. This is why the local church is so important because it gives us all the opportunity to be part of something that corporately can achieve far more than we can individually. What the local church does, when it functions as it should, is to take a group of ordinary people, all subject to their individual attitudes, weaknesses and lifestyle issues and gathers them together and enables them to do the extraordinary.

It is this togetherness that is the key. For us, as believers, to function as we should, we need to be part of a Body and part of a Family and part of an Army. For us to aspire to be Temples of God and part of the Bride of Christ, we need the support of others. The kind of support we need to be the person God has called us to be can best come from the local church, which is why its importance can never be overstated.

Building a Word and Spirit Church

One of the main strengths of great churches all across the world is maintaining balance. Balance is the key to longevity, endurance and long term, lasting success. The great foundational theme of the New Testament Church found in the book of Acts is the Word and the Spirit. The Church was birthed in Acts 2:1-4 by the out-pouring of the Holy Spirit and not just from verses 42-47. Our goal as leaders and Pastors is to emphasise the Spirit and build on the Word. There should be equal emphasis on the Holy Spirit and the Word. Every Holy Spirit activity must be balanced by the Word and not just emotions or feelings.

Pivotal Scriptures

Joel 2:28 (NKJV) - "And it shall come to pass afterward, that I will pour out My Spirit on all flesh; your sons and your daughters shall prophesy, your old men shall dream dreams, your young men shall see visions."

Micah 4:1-2 (Amplified) - [1]But in the latter days it shall come to pass that the mountain of the house of the Lord shall be established as the highest of the mountains; and it shall be exalted above the hills, and peoples shall flow to it. [2]And many nations shall come and say, 'Come, let us go up to the mountain of the Lord, to the house of the God of Jacob, that He may teach us His ways, and we may walk in His paths.' For the law shall go forth out of Zion and the word of the Lord from Jerusalem.

Joel 2 represents a time 800 years before we read of the Acts 2 outpouring of the Holy Spirit. Micah the prophet shows by a prophetic insight that the Church will be the most important place on the earth to be. It will be established. Notice that it is through the Church we are taught His ways (verse 2). The Church is the instrument of God that will bring change in the earth.

The Hebrew word for **_teach_** here is _yaw-raw':_
A primitive root; properly to flow as water (that is, to rain); transitively to lay or throw (especially an arrow, that is, to shoot); figuratively to point out (as if by aiming the finger), to teach: - (+) archer, cast, direct, inform, instruct, lay, shew, shoot, teach (-er, -ing), through.

These two scriptures marry together to bring about a shadow of the New Testament Church and how it ought to operate and function today. As Joel prophetically ushers in the Holy Spirit (seen 800 years later in Acts 2), Micah brings it back to the mountain of the Lord (or the Church) being a place of teaching, where instruction and direction comes from the Word and not just what we feel the Spirit is doing. Being a Word and Spirit church should be a core value in every church today.

Both the Word and the Spirit have power and life, and when these are given a place in our church they save problems and bring life with growth.

Please take time to read the following key scriptures, making special note of the words in italics.

1. **Psalm 18:30** - As for God, his way is perfect; _the word of the LORD is flawless._ He is a shield for all who take refuge in him.
2. **Psalm 33:4** - _For the word of the LORD is right and true._
3. **Psalm 107:20** - _He sent forth his word and healed them,_ He rescued them from the grave.
4. **Psalm 119:16** - I delight in your decrees; _I will not neglect your word._
5. **Psalm 119:28** - My soul is weary with sorrow; _strengthen me according to your word._
6. **Psalm 147:18** - He sends _his word and melts them,_ he stirs up his breezes, and the waters flow.
7. **Isaiah 40:8** - The grass withers and the flowers fall, but the _word of our God stands forever._
8. **John 1:1** - In the _beginning was the Word, and the Word was with God, and the Word was God._
9. **Acts 6:4 (Amplified)** - But we will continue to _devote ourselves steadfastly to prayer and the ministry of the Word._

10. **Acts 13:44** - On the next Sabbath almost *the whole city gathered to hear the word of the Lord.*

11. **Acts 19:20 (Amplified)** - Thus *the Word of the Lord* [concerning the attainment through Christ of eternal salvation in the kingdom of God] *grew and spread and intensified, prevailing mightily.*

12. **Romans 10:8** - But what does it say? "*The word is near you; it is in your mouth and in your heart,*" that is, the word of faith we are proclaiming.

13. **Ephesians 1:13** - And you also were included in Christ when you *heard the word of truth,* the gospel of your salvation. Having believed, you were *marked in him with a seal, the promised Holy Spirit.*

14. **2 Timothy 4:2** - *Preach the Word;* be prepared in season and out of season; correct, rebuke and encourage—with great patience and careful instruction.

15. **Hebrews 4:12** - *For the word of God is living and active.* Sharper than any double-edged sword, it penetrates even to dividing soul and spirit, joints and marrow; it judges the thoughts and attitudes of the heart.

16. **Revelation 19:13** - He is dressed in a robe dipped in blood, and *his name is the Word of God.*

As we read these scriptures we see how important the Word of God and the Holy Spirit are to our lives and churches. Acts 4:31 shows how both the Spirit and the Word work in harmony:

Acts 4:31 (Amplified) - And when they had prayed, the place in which they were assembled was shaken; and *they were all filled with the Holy Spirit,* and they continued to *speak the Word of God* with freedom and boldness and courage.

Ten Commitments Every Pastor Should Make

These should be embedded as core values and be non-negotiable within the framework of your church.

1. We commit to every Holy Spirit activity that is confirmed by the Word of God.
2. We commit to Holy Spirit ministry that operates by the principles of the Word of God.
   Note: Not entertaining fads or movements that try to destroy the ways of the local church. Not taking away from meeting together as one complete body (Ephesians 2:19- 22; 4:1-16; Hebrews 10:23).

3. **We commit to Holy Spirit prophetic words within the Biblical framework.**

   Note: Personal prophecy in your churches should be judged by values 2 or 3. Also, not basing lives on prophetic words, but by God's written word (1 Corinthians 14:3 & 29; Ephesians 6:17; I Thessalonians 5:19-22; 1 Peter 4:10-11).

4. **We commit to Holy Spirit led worship with the Word of God as our scope.**

   Note: Worship is to be done in a Biblical way by the lifting of hands, clapping, dancing and making a joyful noise with instruments and cymbals. It should bring glory to God and not focus on an individual or people (Psalms 47:1 63:4; 96:1; 100:1; 145:21; 147:7; 149:3; 150:3-5).

5. **We commit to Holy Spirit power governed by the Word of God.**

   Note: Praying for the sick, healing without extreme actions like asking people to throw away tablets, and ignoring medical advice. Let every healed person confirm it was a healing, and not making statements like 'By this time next week you will be healed' (James 5:12-15).

6. **We commit to Holy Spirit changes but with a Biblical approach.**

   Note: Change in any church, large or small, should not be a weekly event. It should not be done without wisdom and godly counsel. People soon lose trust in leadership when bad decisions are made. Bad choices will cost you people, respect and eventually the church! If change is needed, ask for guidance on what can be done quickly or slowly (Proverbs 3:21-24).

7. **We commit to Holy Spirit guidance with a Word of God discipline.**

   Note: It's a great thing when the Holy Spirit leads or guides us. But you cannot neglect the discipline of the Word. The Word should endorse what His Spirit is saying and what you are planning on doing. This is important when bringing in new leaders or elders. They must be proven people (Proverbs 3:1-10; Philippians 2:22; 1 Peter 1:7; Colossians 4:11. 1 Timothy 4:6).

8. **We commit to Holy Spirit imagination with the Word of God authority.**

   Note: When it comes to reaching the lost, especially in this generation, it's easy to get caught in the cosmetics of what we do and by doing so neglect the authority of God's Word. The graphics, music, websites, logos and worship band should not be placed above the authority of God's Word.

9. **We commit to Holy Spirit dreams with God's Word backing up that vision.**

   Note: Whatever God has called us to do it must be backed up by the Word of God. Just 'following the Spirit' without the balance of the Word and Godly counsel is reckless and dangerous (1 John 1:3; Luke 14:25-35).

10. **We commit to Holy Spirit revelation, interpreted through the lens of God's Word.**

    Note: There is nothing new under the sun! Any trend or fad that presents itself with 'new revelation' or 'exclusive insights' must be guarded against. As Pastors and leaders we are responsible for holding on to the Word and 'testing' whatever wind of doctrine that presents itself (1 Timothy 2:3-4; 4:16; 2 Timothy 4:3; Titus 1:9).

GREAT DISCIPLINES WE MUST ADHERE TO

These disciplines will help us stay on course when all others crash and crumble. A church that is built upon God's Word and Spirit will stand the test of time.

1. Consistency in personal prayer, fasting and reading the Word. Not for messages or books, but for you as a Pastor. You cannot impart what you do not have.

2. Return to the basics of church and relationships. People are more important than our ministry ambitions.

3. Preach and teach the Word. Pastor Dick Iverson once said, "A good restaurant never needs to advertise, good food brings people in." There are no quick fixes, no great key and no short cuts. Stay on course and build line upon line, in and out of season. The harvest will come.

4. Being continually filled with the Spirit will strengthen you when you feel weak, bring vision when you cannot see, and breathe life into that which is dead. The Spirit of God always brings life and unity.

5. The Word and Holy Spirit should be prerequisite for leadership. In Acts 6 it was a requirement for those who waited on tables! How much more important is it for our leaders and support team to be baptised and daily filled with the Holy Spirit?

CONCLUSION

Being part of MFE is more than just belonging to a religious organisation. It's being linked with brothers and sisters, churches and Pastors of like spirit who are Word and Spirit driven. We are passionate about each aspect of building God's Church which includes raising up leaders, worship teams, relationships, prayer, faith and the prophetic. To do each one of these effectively we need to balance how we emphasise the Word and the Holy Spirit. Only then can we truly build a church that will out-last us and remain until Jesus returns.

1 Corinthians 3:9-11 (NLT) - 9 For we are both God's workers. And you are God's field. You are God's building. 10 Because of God's grace to me, I have laid the foundation like an expert builder. Now others are building on it. But whoever is building on this foundation must be very careful. 11 For no one can lay any foundation other than the one we already have—Jesus Christ.

Chapter 6 – Colin Cooper

The Holy Spirit, Gifts, Prophecy & Presbytery

The doctrine of pneumatology or doctrine of the Holy Spirit is simple yet complex. Correct understanding of pneumatology makes the difference between having a healthy, happy church and the destruction of the church through disillusionment. It is impossible to cover pneumatology in these next few pages, but I will do my best to give a panoramic view on this amazing, incredible and awesome subject.

One of the most misunderstood things about the Holy Spirit is Gifts and Prophecy: for example, the phrase 'message in tongues' is not found in the Bible. 1 Corinthians 12:1 says 'about spiritual gifts brothers I do not want you to become ignorant'. We have become so familiar with the terminology 'gifts of the Spirit' that we think we know all about them; yet in many Charismatic and Pentecostal circles we are actually ignorant about them and have lost the understanding our fathers had.

So the first question is how many gifts of the Spirit are there? Now the average answer would be nine, and here is what they are:

1. Prophecy
2. Tongues
3. Interpretation
4. Word of Knowledge
5. Word of Wisdom
6. Discerning of Spirits
7. Working of Miracles

8.   Gifts of Healing

9.   Faith

To start with, let's look at Prophecy.

PROPHECY

1 Corinthians 14:1 says 'eagerly desire spiritual gifts especially the gift of prophecy'; and verse 3 says 'everyone who prophesies speaks to men for strengthening, encouragement and comfort', so most would believe that God would use the mortal vessel of a man to speak on His behalf to people and the Church. As verse 4 says, "he who prophesies edifies the Church". Would we be happy with this?

Let's move on to Tongues and Interpretation. I was converted into an Assemblies of God, Pentecostal Church. It was a large and thriving one; now some could speak in a tongue and all the congregation would be silent and wait for the interpretation which would be something like this; 'The Lord would speak to you'…etc. So we would hear the mind of the Lord speak to the church. You could hear during the interpretation 'Amen' 'Hallelujah' and 'Praise God' as people felt that the Lord was speaking into their situation. So far, so good? Well actually NO, because we have just stepped outside the Word of God and the Word of God must be the last word on any subject. 'I don't want you to be ignorant concerning the gifts' (1 Corinthians 12:1).

Let me explain. If this was a gift used for a tongue and the interpretation came as a prophecy, then that would only make eight gifts of the Spirit; prophecy is covered on the first gift of the Spirit, where God speaks to man in a message.

If we want to know how God intends us to function we have to look at the law of first mention, i.e. in Genesis we read, "God had one wife for Adam"; that's the law of first mention. One man, one wife. It became distorted later with David having many wives. Concerning the Holy Spirit and Tongues, we go to the law of first mention - 'the disciples were filled with the Holy Spirit' (Acts 21:1-11).

Now there are many different works of the Spirit. In John 20:22 'Jesus breathed on them and they received the Holy Spirit'. But this was not being filled; it was a different work of the Spirit to that in Acts 2 where the disciples spoke in other tongues (v4). But let's look at Acts 2:11 – Jews, Cretans and Arabs heard them *declaring the wonders of God* (not a prophecy) then again in

Acts 10:44-46 'Cornelius and his household were filled with the Spirit' and verse 46 says - 'for they heard them *speaking in tongues and praising God*!

1. Acts 2:4 - Declaring the wonders of God.
2. Acts 10:46 - Praising God.

Both were after being filled with the Spirit, and here was a Tongue which followed.

Now to help us understand a little further, take a look at 1 Corinthians 14:2 – 'For anyone who speaks in a Tongue *does not speak to men* but to God'. Then v3 continues – 'but everyone who prophesies speaks to men'. So there is clear distinction between Prophecy, Tongues and Interpretation.

So a prophecy from God comes to men, but a Tongue interpreted goes to God. For example a prophecy would go something like this:

A – (Prophecy) For the Lord would say to you that I will bless your household etc.

But an Interpretation would sound something like this:

B – (Interpretation) I see the Almighty seated on the throne, filled with majesty etc.

A – Prophecy: <u>God</u> to man

B – Interpretation: <u>Man</u> to God

So if this is the ninth gift working correctly, why has God allowed its dysfunction? Donald Gee, who was one of the Pentecostal fathers, put it like this:

"One of the interesting phenomena of the Pentecostal movement has been the development of this habit of frequent messages in Tongues. The scriptural basis for this is extremely meagre. A message in Tongues is unbiblical, so a better way to put it is an utterance in Tongues.

God's way of speaking to the church is a Tongue-less Prophecy which speaks to man – 1 Corinthians 1:22 'Tongues then are a sign not for believers but for unbelievers'. This scripture is saying it's a mystery where unbelievers are excluded, and of course they are, because they (the unbeliever) could not declare the wonders of God nor could they be praising God.

The habit of giving so many public messages by Tongues and Interpretation has been divinely permitted until a more mature appreciation of the better gifts of the Spirit has been arrived at, through spiritual maturity."

The practice of a message in Tongues was one which the early Pentecostal movement slipped into by virtue of its spiritual immaturity. No doubt this will be rectified as years go by. Many interpretations are prophecies, and the Tongue has freed the faith for the prophecy.

So we have 9 gifts of the Spirit – it would not make sense to have 2 the same. 1 Corinthians 14:7 says about the flute or harp; 'how will anyone know what tune is being played unless there is a distinction in the notes'? It's saying there is a distinct difference between the gifts of Tongues and Prophecy.

So we have briefly looked at Tongues and the correct function, now let's look at Prophecy and the correct function.

Revelation 19:10 says the 'testimony of Jesus is the Spirit of prophecy'. So we must allow the Spirit of Christ to speak through us to His Church. Prophecy is not your mind and vocabulary, but inspired thoughts from God.

The word Prophecy comes from "*prophetevo*" which means to proclaim (not preach). Prophecy is spontaneous, but preaching expounds a prepared text – but both preaching and prophesying are inspired.

There are clearly levels of prophecy in the scripture, so let's look at some now:

1.   1 Corinthians 14:31 says 'all may prophesy'.
2.   1 Corinthians 12:10 talks about the gift of Prophecy.
3.   Ephesians 4:11 speaks about the ministry of the prophet.

A good example is in Acts 21:8-11 where Philip's daughters prophesied. All may prophesy but some have the gift of Prophecy. Note that God did not speak through the daughters about Paul and his future imprisonment. A deeper level of prophecy was needed so in verse 10 a prophet called Agabus came from Judea. His prophecy was much more specific and detailed.

A prophetic utterance belongs to one of four categories:

1. Edification (1 Corinthians 14:3)
2. Exhortation (1 Corinthians 14:3)
3. Comfort (1 Corinthians 14:3)
4. Future Content (Acts 11:27-28)

A prophet may prophesy after waiting for the Lord to place a divine thought in his mind and his responsibility is to judge the thought based on scripture.

Let's briefly look at a higher prophetic flow:

1. The Holy Spirit said (Acts 13:2)
2. The Holy Spirit says (Acts 21:11)
3. The Spirit says (1 Timothy 4:1-5)
4. As the Holy Spirit says (Hebrews 3:7-11)

In Romans 12:6 it directs the prophet to prophesy according to his faith. *A word of warning –* many have prophesied according to what they thought was faith and have been grossly incorrect, leaving damaged lives.

For example, one leader in the church that I pastor became ill with cancer, and people were giving words of prophecy that he would not die. Now it was all done with a good heart and a hope for a complete recovery, but sadly he died.

This could have left family members and the church completely shattered, as I had observed in several other churches in similar situations. So I spoke to the church on a Sunday morning, and telling them the stories of similar situations, I said 'please don't bring any prophecies about healing' – did that seem harsh? I went on to explain that when we love someone we allow our emotions to speak for us without knowing it. Because we want to see our friends and loved ones healed it's hard to separate our desire from the mind of God, and it's difficult to know the difference. Prophecy can also be presumption rather than faith. So, on the death of that leader the church grieved, but was not devastated because the prophecies did not come to pass.

In a recent decade, all the prophecies from major names were examined and it was found that 95% had not come to pass. The difficulty is that few of the givers of prophecy were accountable for the words spoken. I believe everyone that gives prophecies should be brought back to apologise when words spoken have been proven to be totally inaccurate. Even in the ungodly world, systems have regulators to professions giving advice to the public. How much more then should we have accountability for our words and actions that affect lives in a dramatic way!

A proven way for prophets to be accountable to any church wishing to have input with prophecy is to have a presbytery.

PRESBYTERY

The way prophets have functioned in the recent past has roughly been something like this; an individual with a prophetic gift would stand and pick people out of a congregation and prophesy over them, perhaps give a word to the Pastor or the church, then often go away and leave the prophecies in the church to be fulfilled or not. Presbytery is different.

Presbytery is an Ephesians 4 ministry, and the word comes from *presbuteros*, which in Greek signifies an elder or older man. So he must be mature in the natural and the spiritual, not a novice (1 Timothy 3:6). Someone can have a prophetic gift and be a novice, which could be a danger to a church.

GUIDELINES FOR A PRESBYTER

1. He must be part of a local church where his prophecies have been proven, as many prophets have appointed themselves.
2. He must have correct qualifications of his character as in 1 Timothy 3:1-7; a man can be gifted and prophesy, but live a shameful life.
3. He must have a life lived to a high moral standard, so no finger can be pointed at him or disrepute come to the prophetic function and hurt churches.
4. No presbyter should be influenced by financial gain, e.g. selling tickets to hear the prophetic or any monetary reasons. His motive must be pure.
5. A presbyter must have a solid doctrine grounded on the Word and be able to handle scripture in a mature way (1 Timothy 1:18-19, 1 Tim 1:16).

THE FUNCTION OF PRESBYTERY

1. **Presbyters should travel in a recommended group of 3 people for several reasons.**

   A Presbyter, like anyone else, does not have all the gifts (1 Corinthians 12:7 and 11). It also prevents one person being elevated in the eyes of the people. 2 Corinthians 13:1 says – 'the matter is established by 2 or 3 witnesses' - so this is a confirming and agreeing together. A single person has a greater scope for error prophesying by himself.

2. **It would not be recommended that the Presbyters are from the same church that is holding the Presbytery, as they are familiar with the people and the problems.**

   In the scripture generally you find the word prophets – they are found in the plural (Acts 15:22 and 32 – 'chosen men were sent out'). The scripture says 'Judas and Silas who themselves were prophets'.

   In 1 Samuel 19:20 they saw the company of the prophets prophesying; again, plural, which brings security and a greater accuracy as they confer with each other.

3. **Presbyters must be under the local leadership at all times and the local leaders have the final decision and ultimate responsibility before God and the people.**

   Presbyters are not policemen from God telling the leaders what to do and they are not Old Testament prophets.

4. **Old and New Testament prophets – are they the same?**

   Old Testament prophets were judges having responsibility and would bring words of judgement to nations, cities and people. But now we have to take everything through the cross, so today's prophets do not have the responsibility that the Old Testament prophets had. New Testament prophets speak to men for their strengthening, encouragement and comfort. In fact they leave church and individuals blessed. For a man who *claims* to be a prophet and speaks doom and gloom over church or people saying things like – "Sayeth the Lord; 'ICHABOD' is written over this church", lay hands on him suddenly and say "thus sayeth the Lord; you talk a lot of rubbish!"

5. **Church and presbyters prepare by prayer and fasting.**

   This causes our spirits to have a greater sensitivity and prophetic flow in revelation and has benefits to all who get involved.

6. **Choosing those who will be prophesied over** – *did you say choosing?*

Don't prophets prophesy over those they want to? Well, some people have the kind of face that prophets pick on all the time. I have that kind of face – in conferences and other gatherings I can almost guarantee that if there is a prophetic time I will be prophesied over. Not that I mind, but many never get a prophecy because they don't have what I call 'prophegenic' faces. By choosing individuals, the prophets really have to seek the Lord (and likewise the candidate). 1 Timothy 5:22 exhorts us not to lay hands on individuals suddenly.

Make sure they are qualified; and some of those qualifications are being saved, baptised in water, filled with the Spirit, having stable lives, being mature, faithful to the church and submissive to leadership – otherwise the prophetic will frustrate them. Presbytery is not to be used for solving individual's problems or for therapy.

7. **Order of the presbytery.**

Each prophet will prophesy in turn over the individuals. It's best not to ask God to speak on a subject but let God speak on what He wants to speak on.

When the prophets stop speaking, all the presbyters will lay hands on the candidates and pray with them.

The prophets will only prophesy if there is a prophetic mantle on them. If that mantle departs they will stop prophesying, as prophecy cannot be forced. If the mantle is strong and the flow is powerful, scripture says that we can all prophesy, but the church members must resist this and allow the prophets alone to function in this realm as seasoned prophets. Sometimes they may speak prophetic words to people in the congregation.

8. **How do we choose individuals for presbytery?**
   a. The leader chooses, because he knows the sheep.
   b. Some apply for this ministry by asking or writing to the leader but the leader will make the final decision.
   c. If the person chosen does not wish to go through presbytery, then no pressure should be put on them.
   d. Start with the main leaders, then eventually over the years every member can go through presbytery.

The individuals who go through presbytery have a responsibility to press into God during the worship time, and focus on worshipping the Lord with intensity. As Revelation 2:7 says – "he who has an ear let him hear what the Spirit says to the churches". Worship can bring down a prophetic mantle; when Elisha prophesied in 2 Kings 3:11 he first asked for a harpist to play and then he prophesied. Then in Samuel 10:5-10 it talks about a company of prophets, and walking with them were musicians.

The presbytery gathering is different from the normal church service. We read in Joel 1:14 and 2:15 that when the people came together it was called a season of sacred assembly. Although it starts with worship, there is no set order and no regular pattern, so a greater sensitivity to the Spirit is needed as anything can happen. The congregation should have been prepared for presbytery by fasting one or two days a week for approximately six weeks beforehand and those going through presbytery should do the same but with an extra couple of days if possible right up to the day before the gathering, as fasting gives all a greater sensitivity.

After correct preparation by the entire congregation there will be a rising expectation and increasing flow of the felt presence of the Lord. The presbyters will then move into speaking the preached Word or they may immediately begin the prophetic ministry: or prophetic ministry first then the Word; or perhaps no Word at all. After each chosen individual or couple have received presbytery, it is good to sing songs.
That will be conducive to allowing the mantle to flow.

A Word Of Warning On Presbytery

This should never be exercised in a house group or any group that has no proven prophets. There needs to be authority where there is accountability; no one should 'have a go' at presbytery. Only those who have been schooled and proven should conduct such a gathering as immense harm can be done to groups and individuals. Done with sensitivity and levelheaded balance, presbytery can move the whole church forward.

Encourage all in the congregation to participate in worship as human nature, which is inquisitive, will be looking around and spectating rather than worshipping. A novelty factor can cause people to watch, it's a responsibility and a discipline to worship fervently.

In David and Solomon's tabernacle the Levites were appointed to record prophecies, utterances and songs (1 Chronicles 16). So have the modern day scribes record all of them.

A Reminder About Prophetic Utterances

1. All prophecy is conditional. It is never to be a replacement for, or carry the same authority, as God's written Word. Nor must it contradict the written Word. Scripture tells us in 1 Peter 1:25 "we have the Word which is more sure, it stands forever". Of course if the individual lives a loose, ungodly lifestyle then they could miss out and lose the prophetic words given.

2. Presbytery can only function if there is unity in the house. Remember, it is not for settling church problems and disputes.

3. The whole church can receive a fresh vision and momentum. Many churches, including the one I am based in, began to grow after a presbytery.

4. A prophetic word given to an individual can leapfrog into someone else's heart when we are correctly prepared spiritually.

5. Presbytery is generally a once in a lifetime experience. It's recommended that married couples go through presbytery together. Unless there is an exceptional reason for a young, single person to go through, he or she should wait until God brings their future partner to them, then they can go through together. Of course older singles with no partner can be candidates.

6. Presbytery is a confirming nature which can validate the leadership's thoughts of individuals and cause rejoicing at the illumination of the minds of the leaders.

7. Do not try and force fulfilment of the utterances.

Prophetic utterances fall into four categories:

1. **The past.** Revealed to let the candidate know God is on his case, although nothing would be spoken to embarrass him, only to encourage. We understand the past because we have been there.

2. **The present.** We can see what we hear because we are living in it, and it confirms what God is speaking.

3. **The future.** We can see in part what the prophet spoke about, and it's confirmation to the leaders of the house about a gifting, a plan or a position. It has great credibility; it has clarified his purpose.

4.   **The future**. A mystery we can't understand, see or work it out. Take the word and put it on a spiritual shelf, and the Lord can work it out in His own time.

I have been around for a long time. When the young people find out that I was converted as a teenager in the mid-60s, they think I am a fossil; but I have been alive long enough to know that some Christians are lazy and think the prophetic will give a quick fix. "Do it now God," they cry, and they can get depressed because it's been a long time since the prophetic utterance was given. "It's been 6 weeks now and nothing has happened!" Well let me tell you, I was given a prophetic word 22 years ago and it's coming to pass only now.

Scripture says in Ephesians 5:17 "don't be foolish but understand what the Lord's will is". There is no substitute for reading the Word and seeking the face of God in prayer. A man who is not baptised in the Spirit will be more effective than one who is when he lives in the Word and seeks the face of God, but the man who is filled with the Spirit, reads the Word and seeks the face of God will be incredibly effective. Colossians 1:9 – "since the day we heard about you we have not stopped praying for you and asking God to fill you with the knowledge of His will through all spiritual wisdom and understanding".
Seek God with all your heart, mind and Spirit. Then the Lord will be very willing to reveal His incredible will to you.

So then presbytery has incredible benefits:

1.   Helps individuals find their function in the house.
2.   Confirms God's will.
3.   Strengthens individuals.
4.   Strengthens the whole church.
5.   Raises the spiritual level of the church.
6.   Deposits faith in the heart of the congregation.
7.   Gives the church understanding of the prophetic flow.
8.   Confirms ministries by the laying on of hands.
9.   The church receives spiritual direction through the prophetic.
10. The church has a better understanding of the local church authority.
11. Causes a joy and excitement in the body.

In both the Old and New Testaments joy is consistently the mark of a believer. It's not just an emotion, but a quality, a fruit of life worked out in the Lord. Psalm 16:11 says – "there is joy in

Your presence". Presbytery brings in the joy of the Lord. "May the God of hope fill you with all joy and peace as you trust in Him so that you may overflow with hope" (Romans 15:13).

By the power of the Spirit - All this flows from being filled continually with the Holy Spirit. It is essential to keep filled.

1 Thessalonians 5:16 - "be joyful always." It is possible in adversity to keep filled.

Philippians 4:4 - "Rejoice in the Lord always and again I say rejoice".

John 15:9-11 - "Obey Him and your joy will be complete".

Happy churches see souls saved and the prophetic flow continues the spirit of the joy of the Lord. Joylessness can come when we abuse the Holy Spirit and forget He is a person; this then stops the prophetic flow.

Let's remind ourselves of the Word:

1.   The Holy Spirit can be grieved - Ephesians 4:30
2.   He can be insulted - Hebrews 10:29
3.   He can be quenched - 1 Thessalonians 5:19.
4.   Grieved and vexed - Isaiah 63:10.
5.   He can be lied to - Acts 5:3.
6.   Also blasphemed - Matthew 12:31-32.
7.   And even tested - Acts 5:9.
8.   And resisted - Acts 7:51.

Any one of these 8 terrible things can prevent the spirit of joy in the house of the Lord.

So, my friends, presbytery, the prophets and all the joy that goes with it is part of the Lord bringing back the work of the Dove in the house. Acts 15:15-18 tells us that His Church is being restored, that the Dove is returning once again to His house and that we are the only hindrance. 2 Peter 3:12 tells us that we can speed the day of the Lord; we speed its coming. The Holy Spirit working through presbytery is one more ingredient of that great and glorious day.

MIXING THE SEED

Mixing the seed is a very important subject when we look at church growth. Some churches remain weak despite being involved in citywide campaigns, even when they are an integral part of such campaigns. These churches want as much blessing as possible from other groups, churches or organisations, and their motto is 'the more the merrier'. These churches are faithful in attending conferences, and attend as many as possible to receive blessing from as wide a range of churches as they possibly can.

As Pastors we have great information on topics including church building, winning souls for Jesus, anointing, teamwork, preaching, worship, pastoring and prayer. We put much of what we have learned into practice and let it do its work: faith and expectation is high that results will come. Years later we look back on what we have done and find that there is no growth, and indeed it sometimes seems that the church has taken a step backward: what went wrong? We have all this information and lots of contacts in other churches and organisations but still no breakthrough. How can this be?

The key to the answer is found in:

Deuteronomy 22:9 (NIV) - "Do not plant two kinds of seed in your vineyard; if you do, not only the crops you plant but also the fruit of the vineyard will be defiled."

A good farmer would not plant barley and wheat together, or turnips with potatoes, even though they are similar crops. If the farmer did plant barley and wheat together he would find that the wheat interfered with the growth of the barley, and the barley with the growth of the wheat. The ultimate result would be a weak harvest.

The same principle applies in family life. I have a natural family consisting of my wife Sue, two children and a few grandchildren. If my wife asked me where I was going and I said 'to the Jones family', and then the next day said 'to the Smith family', my family would be unhappy and confused. My wife would be very hurt, my children would be unhappy and my grandchildren would look at me with dismay, and this would all be perfectly understandable.

If I really lived like this I would not be able to build and care for my family effectively. How do I really care for my family? I do it by putting all my effort, energy, commitment, finances and love into my one family. I do not give all these things to other families even though I relate to other families around me. I have one family where my children receive teaching, correction and rebuke from one father: if my children received teaching and correction from many fathers it would cause great confusion to them.

Just as this principle applies in the natural world of crops and families so it also applies in the spiritual world. It is the same with our spiritual families. Today there are many spiritual voices saying many things: who should we listen to? Just as being in one human family is the correct way, so one spiritual family is God's way when we put our spiritual roots down.

Psalm 46:4 (NIV) - "There is a river whose streams make glad the city of God, the holy place where the Most High dwells."

The river represents the spirit of the Lord, and it flows through the city, which is representative of the church, so when we firmly put our roots down in the church we will be in the place where His spirit makes our heart glad.

Psalm 52:8 (NIV) - "But I am like an olive tree flourishing in the house of God; I trust in God's unfailing love for ever and ever."

This verse says that we will be like olive trees flourishing in the house of God. In Isaiah 55:12 we read of the trees of the field clapping their hands. I have looked at many trees in my lifetime: big ones, small ones, tall ones and broad ones. I have seen flowers, buds, branches, leaves and fruit but never have I seen hands attached to the trees, clapping. When the Bible talks of trees it is referring to people.

Using the analogy of trees, the root is where a person gets his or her nourishment from and this is where he or she is planted. The trunk speaks to us of a person's character which is developed from the root and is the source of all his instruction. Upon this depends the type of fruit that the person produces, and whether it is good or bad, plentiful or limited. We can see from this that where a person is planted is extremely important.

Psalm 92:12-14 (NIV) - "The righteous will flourish like a palm tree, they will grow like a cedar of Lebanon; planted in the house of the LORD, they will flourish in the courts of our God. They will still bear fruit in old age, they will stay fresh and green,"

Scripture states that the righteous will flourish planted like a palm tree, they will grow like a cedar of Lebanon planted in the house of the Lord, and they will flourish in the courts of God. Verse 14 says that if we are living with our roots in one garden we will still be effective and fresh even when we get old.

There is an increasing trend today for leaders in the Kingdom to network. The Oxford Concise Dictionary defines networking as "Intersecting horizontal and vertical lines like the structure of a net - a group of people exchanging information, contacts and experience for professional or social purposes establishing new links."

One business professional said to me "wherever I go I leave my card and email address because some of these people could one day be a benefit to me." I often observe Christian leaders doing exactly the same thing; handing out cards and attending various conferences in order to be seen and recognised, hoping that the leaders of that conference will one day be a benefit to them. When there is a response from such new contacts the leaders start to put their time and energy into the new group.

It is always nice to meet new people and generally we are given a lot of attention because we are new, and we all like being fussed over. The process is like a honeymoon: we slowly get to know each other, but eventually we find that the knight in shining armour that the bride fell in love with, and his beautiful white horse, is not actually as perfect as she thought. The armour has become a bit rusty and the horse leaves manure all over the place; the bride ends up doing a lot of cleaning up! It takes a minimum of five years to really get to know a person so my advice is to stay in the field where the Lord has planted you, and sow your seed from the fruit that you produce in that field.

Networking is simply trying to use people for personal benefit, and it is hard to fully trust a leader who tries to sow in many fields, rather than concentrating on his own. Proverbs 11:3 says that the unfaithful are destroyed by their duplicity.

Relationships are vital in building anything, be it churches, organisations or conferences. Nothing works long term without dependable, faithful and trusting relationships. I have had cases of men pledging their faithfulness to me but who then left me for a new opportunity when one came along which looked better in their eyes. Proverbs 20:6 says, "many claim to have unfailing love but a faithful man who can find?" Paul understood this when he wrote in Philippians 2:20-21 that Timothy is genuine and has a real, pure interest in others, but the average person has his own interest at heart.

I would just say this: decide which field you are going to sow into and be faithful to that. There is strength when we are together. Ecclesiastes 4:9-12 clearly speaks about the fact that we will achieve more by not spreading our seed thinly. In Genesis 14:8-16 we read about four kings who seize all of the goods of Sodom and Gomorrah and carry off Abram's nephew, Lot, and his possessions. Abram took only 318 men from his household and routed the four kings and their kingdoms. From this we can see the great effect that a small group working in unity can have, defeating many times their number. I would rather work with men and women who are dedicated to working with each other and sowing in the same field. You can achieve more with a group of fifty who are with you, and sowing in the same field, than you can with a thousand who are not wholly with you. Proverbs 12:26 says that you should choose your friends carefully, but choose and then give your all. Sow good seeds and have a strong harvest.

How do we know which field we should sow into? It all comes down to trust, and trust is a voluntary action.

1. **Trust is a choice.**
   Work hard to develop friendships and sow into relationships in the field that you choose.

2. **Trust is an attitude.**
   How we sow affects the way that we live, and an attitude of trust affects our behaviour.

3. **Trust is a risk.**
   Because I cannot carry the seed bag all by myself, my life is always part of other people's lives, and I am in their hands and need to trust them.

4. **Trust is not a conditional relationship.**

We do not have contingency plans in case conditions change. When we sow together we will receive a harvest, and even if we are disappointed, relationships can be worked out if we are willing.

5. **Trust will cost.**

It costs me to lay down my own personal will; it costs me to be vulnerable. Sometimes we are too concerned about being strong and looking like what we think we should look like.

6. **Trust is to be trustworthy ourselves.**

In Philippians 2:22 Paul says that Timothy has proved himself loyal and faithful, but Proverbs 25:27 says that it is not honourable to seek our own honour. Choose where you will sow. Plant yourself and be faithful to those you work with and reap a strong church, a good harvest and good relationships. Even when we stand together to sow, we will still have troubles, but Proverbs 17:17 says, "a friend loves at all times and a brother is born for trouble."

7. **Trust is reliability.**

2 Timothy 2:2 encourages us to commit whatever we do to faithful men who will teach others. Reliable men will sow seeds into others. If we are not dependable to the men and women we walk with then we will not be trusted with greater responsibility. Matthew 25:21 describes this principle. Luke 16:10-13 clearly speaks about serving 2 seeds: you cannot do it effectively. It speaks about being reliable with someone else's ministry, whether a Pastor, conference organiser or denomination; reliability is the cornerstone of a good harvest.

8. **Trust is consistency.**

Consistency is almost like reliability but the difference is that that we have a passion for what we do that is unchanging: it will be exactly the same tomorrow as it is today. Scripture says that God is not man, He is not like shifting sand, but He is the same yesterday, today and tomorrow. Consistency means that we sow our seed consistently in the field and we do not look for an exit if we do not get our own way: we have an absolutely dependable spirit so that those we work with know that no matter what comes we will be with them in the good times and the bad. Inconsistency is hard on relationships and it is hard to work with an inconsistent person.

9. **Trust is not about feelings.**

Trust is a determination to fulfil the promise we gave. It is not leaving to go to another field if I feel rejected, only staying if it is convenient for me; this is a short-term mentality. Those leaders who stay together the longest have the greatest impact on the world. I am sure that it would be generally agreed that Billy Graham and his team have had a bigger impact on the world with the gospel than most ministries, and I believe that this is due to the longevity of the relationship he has had with Beverly Shea and Cliff Barrows; they have been together since the 1940's. They have been consistent in the field that they sowed into. Friends who stay and work together long-term are secure with each other. We need to decide which field we are to sow into and not get mystical in asking to God to move us. Short-term thinkers are never secure with each other.

So my friends do not mix the seed: sow in only one field so that we might harvest an excellent crop of souls in a dying world.

Chapter 8 — Gordon Tose

Church Government

I became a Christian in my early thirties from a totally non-church background and as I started church life I naively assumed that people who went to church were obviously Christians. Why else would they go to church? Of course if they were Christians they were automatically nice people doing their level best to live their lives in accordance with the Word of God. Reality came as a bit of a shock to me.

I began my church life in a sleepy little market town where the only two churches of any note were both denominational churches. I remember being taught at one of the midweek Bible studies (from Matthew 7) that it was wrong to judge people and that I should pay more attention to the plank of wood in my own eye rather than worry about the speck of sawdust in my brother's eye. How this worked out was that if people decided to do the "wrong thing" then that was up to them and we shouldn't judge them; far better to let God sort them out in His own good time. I wasn't too surprised then when nothing was done to support the ministers of these two churches who ended up having nervous breakdowns because of conflicts with certain factions within their congregations.

A short time later my wife and I left the church. I remember thinking "there must be more to Christianity than this". This may have been a bit harsh but it's how I felt at the time, and we joined a small charismatic church with a membership of about thirty adults. Within a month of us joining the new church, half of the members left following a disagreement with the eldership and I was beginning to wonder about the desirability of church life. We stayed at that church for about a year before my job moved me on, but one of the things I remember about that year was all the reports of disputes within other churches similar to ours. Not just disputes but real conflicts within the leadership teams resulting in church splits.

My job brought me to Huddersfield where we joined Huddersfield Christian Fellowship. That was 20 years ago and we have been there ever since. Up until that time there were two things in life that I avoided like the plague. One was public speaking and the other was confrontation, and I have to confess that all this conflict that I had observed in my brief church life had unsettled me. I did, however, recall my earlier instruction "not to judge" and I was confident that God would indeed sort things out when the time was right.

Two years later I found myself guarding the front entrance of the church with five other men behind me, and I emphasise the fact that they were behind me, not in front of me. I was eyeballing one of the church elders refusing him and his family entry. So I found myself, someone who would do anything to avoid confrontation, in this incredibly uncomfortable role of church bouncer. Looking back, I would have to say that this was probably one of the worst times of my life, and yet what it did was to give me the realisation that government was actually an integral part of church life. Whilst Jesus' command to us "do not judge" is valid within the right context, equally valid are the Apostle Paul's comments:

1 Corinthians 5:3-5 (NIV) - "Even though I am not physically present, I am with you in spirit. And I have already passed judgement on the one who did this, just as if I were present. When you are assembled in the name of our Lord Jesus and I am with you in spirit, and the power of our Lord Jesus is present, hand this man over to Satan, so that the sinful nature may be destroyed and his spirit saved on the day of the Lord"

Paul finishes chapter 5 with these words:-

"What business is it of mine to judge those outside the church? Are you not to judge those inside? God will judge those outside. Expel the wicked man from among you".

There is a scripture in Judges 17:6 and it is repeated word for word in Judges 21:25 and it says, *"In those days, Israel had no king, everyone did as he saw fit."* In other words there was no authority and people took advantage of the situation, which is what people do whether they are Christians or not. The reality is that for people to behave as they should, they need authority. We see the truth of this in our schools, in our homes and in our places of work and church is no different: without a structure of authority, people, including Christians, think they can say and do what they want, when they want.

Of course the events of the Book of Judges took place three thousand years ago and we may think they have little relevance to our churches today. However, a cursory glance at the New Testament churches shows that nothing much had changed. In the Corinthian church there was division, there was immorality and the abuse of communion. In the second letter to the Corinthians we see that people were slandering Paul. There were ambitious and divisive Christians in the church at Ephesus as well as false teaching, which also occurred in the church at Galatia and Colosse. In the second letter to Timothy the Apostle Paul writes about disputes, divisions and worldliness in the Church generally and the truth is that people do not change. What was true of people in the Book of Judges and at the time of the Apostle Paul is true of people today. The experience of division that I have witnessed personally and have heard about from all over the world are really echoes of Paul's words to the Ephesians, to whom he writes:

Acts 20:29-31 (NIV) - "I know that after I leave, savage wolves will come in among you and will not spare the flock. Even from your own number men will arise and distort the truth in order to draw away disciples after them. So be on your guard."

It has been my experience that the root of division is pride and the manifestation of pride is ambition, and pride is at the very heart of man. Looking at the scripture in Acts 20, what we are seeing is the New Testament equivalent of the "Absalom Spirit". What we see wonderfully described in 2 Samuel 15:1-12 is Absalom raising himself up, giving himself a platform, or more accurately abusing the platform he already had, and drawing men to himself.

In my experience Absaloms are always two things. Firstly they are generally nice people, the kind of people that other people readily take to their hearts. They are quick to show their concern for others. Of course if they were not nice then other people would not be taken in by them. If they had two horns and a tail, which is what they should have, then they would fool nobody. Secondly, Absaloms are usually gifted people: gifted and nice is a powerful combination either for good or for evil.

However if we look at Acts 20:28 we would see that Paul doesn't just say:

"Keep watch over the flock of which the Holy Spirit has made you overseers"

He also says:

"Keep watch over yourselves"

Let us not forget to whom he is writing; he is writing to the Ephesian elders, he is writing to their leaders. Verse 30:

"even from your own number men will arise"

It is my contention that this statement can be taken as "even from within your own leadership team men will arise". Absalom already had a position of influence, he was the king's son, and Absaloms that cause the real trouble and the real heartache and the real damage are not generally sitting in the congregation, they are sitting in the leadership meetings. Of course we will look at ourselves and think that we could never be an Absalom, in which case we need to heed Paul's words:

1 Corinthians 10:12 (NIV) - "So, if you think you are standing firm, be careful you don't fall"

Whilst this may sound a bit pessimistic, it is not as pessimistic as:

Proverbs 20:6 (Good News):-"Everyone talks about how loyal and faithful he is, but just try and find someone who really is".

The unfortunate reality is that for church to be as church was meant to be, there has to be an authority structure in operation which is not afraid to exercise Biblically based government. Of course this raises various questions. How do we exercise this authority? How do we maintain Biblical standards in church? How do we dispense Godly discipline? The Apostle Paul answers these questions in part by likening the relationship between leader and congregation to that of a parent to their children.

1 Thessalonians 2:11-12 (NIV) - "For you know that we dealt with each of you as a father deals with his own children, encouraging, comforting and urging you to live lives worthy of God, who calls you into his kingdom and glory".

When God created the family his intention was that the children should be raised by two parents, a father and a mother, who would bring balance to the family unit. One of the reasons that there are so many problems in our society today is because as the traditional family unit breaks down, and more and more children are raised by a single parent, so the balance in raising them is wrong. In the context of church, that is why *team* is important as it brings balance in the process of raising our congregation. I sometimes think that calling ourselves "Pastors" can be a bit misleading because not everyone who occupies the office of Pastor actually has the Ephesians 4 ministry of Pastor. The bigger the team, and the more varied the giftings within it, the greater the chance of success in producing a spiritually mature congregation.

As a parent the main motivation behind our leadership should be love. I love my two sons and in that I am no different to the overwhelming majority of fathers. I want the best for them, I always have and I always will, but when they were children I knew that the "best for them" wasn't always letting them have their own way and an important part of raising children is discipline.

Hebrews 12:6 (NIV) - "The Lord disciplines those he loves".

Discipline, which is the exercise of authority, should always come out of a heart of love and never out of a heart of anger. I appreciate that this is easier said than done because some of the people that God entrusts us with appear at times almost more trouble than they are worth. We have been glad to see the back of some people who have left church over the years because they could not get their own way, or because it became clear to them that their own personal ambitions and agendas were not going to be met. I have always felt sadness at their leaving because I think what might have been achieved if only the problem or the issue could have been overcome. I dwell on what they could have achieved both for themselves and the church if only they had been willing to submit to the control that was being put on them.

The main reason for discipline is to protect and again this is a parental role, and when I think of protection I think of four distinct areas:

Firstly there is the need to protect the guilty from themselves. I love Paul's admonition of the Cretan Christians in Titus 1:12-13. How many potentially good Christians have ruined themselves because no one had the courage to confront them about their behaviour? I have found over the years that most people do not like confrontation, and nor should they. Disliking it, however, is no excuse to avoid it. The problem with avoiding it is that generally the problem does not go away, in fact it usually gets worse, and in the process the ones causing the problems fail to fulfil their potential in God. That is very sad.

When it comes to protecting people from themselves we automatically think of restoration and our thoughts go to scriptures like:

Galatians 6:1 (NIV) - "Brothers if someone is caught in a sin, you who are spiritual should restore him gently"

The emphasis here is on the word "gently". Sometimes the only thing that gets through to some people is a spiritual smack. Nevertheless we should always be ready to extend mercy and forgiveness.

2 Corinthians 2:5-8 (NIV) - "If anyone has caused grief, he has not so much grieved me as he has grieved all of you, to some extent - not to put it too severely. The punishment inflicted on him by the majority is sufficient for him. Now instead, you ought to forgive and comfort him, so that he will not be overwhelmed by excessive sorrow. I urge you therefore to reaffirm your love for him".

However we should not rely on that kind of scripture if all we are doing is using it to avoid the need for confrontation.

Secondly there is the need to protect the church. It is one thing to focus on the restoration of the sinner but equally valid is the protection of the other members of the church. They too need protection, not only from the effects of the sin but also from the influence of the sin.

1 Corinthians 5:6 (NIV) - "Don't you know that a little yeast works through the whole batch of dough?"

Sin which is left unchecked and unchallenged is dangerous, not just for the individual but for the church as a whole, because there is always the risk of others doing outwardly what they have only been tempted to do inwardly when they see someone else getting away with it.

Thirdly discipline protects the reputation of the church and therefore the honour of God. It is a fact that when children misbehave it is not just the children themselves who are disapproved of but also their parents. I appreciate that at some stage in their development children have to take responsibility for their own actions but, rightly or wrongly, when the child messes up, society tends to hold the parents partly responsible. Just as in the natural so it is in the spiritual, and when God's children mess up it is the family home, the church, which is brought into disrepute and the Father is dishonoured.

Romans 2:23-24 (NIV) - "You who brag about the law, do you dishonour God by breaking the law? As it is written: God's name is blasphemed among the Gentiles because of you."

Fourthly there is the need to protect the Pastor himself. It is a Biblical principle to honour the Father of the House and of course this is achieved in a variety of ways. One way of honouring is to protect him and this is where "team" comes in. It is impractical, and in some cases inadvisable, to say that the Senior Pastor should never be involved in disciplinary matters. However there are many cases when he does not need to be involved in disciplinary matters. This is an example of the outworking of the "Jethro principle" in Exodus 18 when Jethro, Moses' father-in-law, told Moses to delegate more before the workload burnt him out. Nothing else grinds you down more than conflict within the church, and if the team can help take that particular burden off of the Pastor's shoulders then obviously the Pastor benefits. As a general principle, when the Pastor benefits, the church benefits, and we see this in Hebrews 13:17. When someone in the church has a problem with the Pastor personally then it is inadvisable that the Pastor should have to deal with that himself.

What it comes down to is that people are people and basically they will do what they feel they want to do. All we can do as leaders is to govern wisely, and this is what we must strive to do. The consequences of governing without wisdom are that we can bring disaster on somebody's walk with God. Dealing with a situation too harshly can destroy someone and being too soft risks them committing spiritual suicide: either way the end result is spiritual death.

Hebrews 13:17 (NIV) - "Obey your leaders and submit to their authority. They keep watch over you as men who must give an account. Obey them so that their work will be a joy, not a burden, for that would be of no advantage to you".

There are three parts to this verse and it is usually the first part that gets most of the attention:

"Obey your leaders and submit to their authority"

However it is the second part of the verse that, over the years, has exercised my mind:

"They keep watch over you as men who must give an account"

It is a great privilege to be a leader in God's house, but with great privilege comes great responsibility. As leaders we will be held responsible for how we lead and if we lead with wisdom then the sheep will be held responsible for how they follow. The third part of the verse is:

"Obey them so that their work will be a joy, not a burden, for that would be of no advantage to you"

This says that where there is good government, in other words Biblical government, then there is order which then brings security. Secure sheep are happy sheep and when the sheep are happy, we as leaders are happy.

BUILDING A GIVING CHURCH

The greatest act of selfless giving is seen in John 3:16 "For God so loved the world that He *gave* His one and only son..." Giving is close to the heart of God and it should be close to our heart. The church, being the bride of Christ, should represent the heart of Jesus.

Proverbs 11:25 (NIV) - A generous man will prosper; he who refreshes others will himself be refreshed.

Let's, for the purpose of application, take out the word 'man' and instead put in 'church.' This is how it would read...

"A generous *church* will prosper; *a church that refreshes* others will itself be refreshed."

All Pastors and leaders everywhere would love to have a prosperous church, a church that is flourishing, taking ground and reaching souls. One of the key ingredients of building a great church is 'giving.' Giving is not exclusive to the 'so called' rich churches or to those who can afford it, or to those churches in richer countries. Giving should be one of the main ingredients of churches everywhere. Remember God is our source and not man.

The book of Acts is the benchmark for all churches everywhere. The book of Acts church was a giving church, so much so, it was even reflected in the people who attended that church.

Acts 4:32-35 (NLT) - [32] All the believers were united in heart and mind. And they felt that what they owned was not their own, so they shared everything they had. [33] The apostles testified powerfully to the resurrection of the Lord Jesus, and God's great blessing was upon them all. [34]

There were no needy people among them, because those who owned land or houses would sell them [35] and bring the money to the apostles to give to those in need.

So as the church grew closer to God through the Holy Spirit, giving became part of the people's lives. They did not need to do a special offering or a fundraiser - the people just gave! When people see God's work being done they will give to the work of the Lord.

Exodus 36:3-7 (NLT) - [3] Moses gave them the materials donated by the people of Israel as sacred offerings for the completion of the sanctuary. But the people continued to bring additional gifts each morning. [4] Finally the craftsmen who were working on the sanctuary left their work. [5] They went to Moses and reported, "The people have given more than enough materials to complete the job the LORD has commanded us to do!" [6] So Moses gave the command, and this message was sent throughout the camp: "Men and women, don't prepare any more gifts for the sanctuary. We have enough!" So the people stopped bringing their sacred offerings. [7] Their contributions were more than enough to complete the whole project.

One of the truths of leadership is this "As the Pastor and leaders, so the people." In other words if you as the Pastor and leaders are givers then the people will be as well.

Here are some truths about prosperous churches that give.

THEY ARE ALWAYS PLANTING SEED

Our churches should be places where all kinds of needs are met, spiritual as well as physical. One of the strengths of churches is that we help and bless those around us. Our churches grow and prosper when we give. Giving should be seen as planting seeds. The Bible tells us in Ephesians 6:7 "people (or churches) reap whatever they sow." Great churches are giving churches. Churches that prosper are churches that sow seeds in and out of season. It is only a foolish farmer that asks for a harvest that he did not plant, or goes to a field to reap where he did not sow. Giving churches prosper because they plant seeds and have many streams of harvest coming in.

Luke 12:20-21 (Amplified) - [20] But God said to him, You fool! This very night they [the messengers of God] will demand your soul of you; and all the things that you have prepared, whose will they be? [21] so it is with the one who continues to lay up and hoard possessions for himself and is not rich [in his relation] to God [this is how he fares].

They Choose the Right Soil

Before any seed is planted the farmer will need to know the quality of the soil he has. When we plant seed as a church, as Pastors and leaders we are responsible for knowing what type of soil we are sowing into. Because of the value of the seed, the farmer knows that careful inspection and testing of that soil must take place before the seed is planted.

Organisations and good causes are ready and equipped to take seed from you at a moment's notice, but these 'different types of soils' must be a place where relationships are flowing between you and the head of that group, also there must be accountability factors in place as to where the seed goes and what it is used for.

The best way to identify all this is to find out whether or not it lines up with God's plan on the earth, which is local church. Para-church organisations are everywhere, but we are to build where God is building and sow where God expects a harvest. That place is church (Matthew 16:13-19; Mark 4:3-9; Acts 20:35; 2 Corinthians 9:1-6).

They Give out Of Faith More Than Finances

Hebrews 11 is known as 'the great faith chapter.' This chapter includes the 'who's who' in faith. But what most scholars and people fail to see is that without obedience there will be no faith. In Hebrews 11:6, it says "And without faith it is impossible to please God." All the great names that we read about in Hebrews 11, and the things that these people did, required obedience to God before they actually saw the reward (Hebrews 11:13-16).

Sometimes we are called to give what we as a church may need at that very moment, but trusting God first will bring rewards. Great churches that prosper are those who give generously, taking of what they themselves need and blessing others. As we do that we scatter seeds that will bring a great harvest back our way. It's all about faith, not the money, not the economy, not where we live or the level of jobs the people in our church have, but faith in God. **Mark 11:22** "Have faith in God." Or literally, "Have the God kind of Faith." Giving is a lifestyle and not an amount, it is not a gifting and it is not just for a season but part of the normal church life.

THEY KNOW THAT GIVING IS A SIGN OF UNITY

Giving exposes the heart of a church, the people and its leadership. If the people are with you then their money will be as well: giving is an issue of the heart.

Matthew 6:21 (NLT) - "Wherever your treasure is, there the desires of your heart will also be."

Before someone leaves your church you will see it first in their giving. People work hard to earn money and when they feel they are no longer with you, the first thing to leave is their money. Building unity is the first step to building a giving church. It's not about preaching on money every week, or asking Pastors to come in and teach on finances, although these have their place. It's more about creating a spirit of unity.

Psalm 133 tells us that where there is unity God commands a blessing, and even life forever more. Unity is contagious, life-giving and a joy to be around. But creating unity will take work, discipline, vision and the Holy Spirit.

Here are some focal points for creating unity:

1. Focus on Jesus and not money (2 Corinthians 4:16-18; Colossians 3:23-25).
2. Focus on His Kingdom living over the culture of the people (Matthew 6:33; 1 Corinthians 12:13; Galatians 3:28).
3. Focus on Giving rather than receiving (Acts 20:35; Luke 6:38; 2 Corinthians 9:6-10).
4. Focus on Relationships rather than gifts (I John 1:3; I Thessalonians 5:12).
5. Focus on Souls rather than numbers (Proverbs 11:30; Luke 15:7).
6. Focus on Generosity rather than being frugal (Proverbs 11:24-25; I Chronicles 29:9).
7. Focus on the People rather than ministry (Matthew 14:14-16; John 21:15-16).
8. Focus on Needs rather than wants (Acts 4:32- 35; Acts 5:12-16).
9. Focus on Church rather than projects (Matthew 16:13-19; Acts 9:1-5).
10. Focus on Sowing rather than reaping (Psalms 126:6; Isaiah 61:3).

THEY BUILD GENEROSITY FROM DAY ONE

To build any great church, there must be a set of principles and guides established that is your DNA as a church and that are non-negotiable values. These should be set out in a class format where new people to your church are taught over a number of weeks what you believe, practise and expect from them. Great churches will instil these beliefs into every potential member of their church.

You should never be afraid to address finances in church; Jesus talked more about money than He did about heaven and hell. Money is close to everyone's heart, especially churches. We all need money to live, to extend, and to take ground. The Bible tells us "money answers all things." (Ecclesiastes 10:19)

Developing a giving church begins by cultivating a giving people. The church membership classes are a period where these truths can be instilled before a new person or people ever join the church. In these classes you can cover issues of the heart when it comes to money and giving, for example: Tithing, Offerings, Special Offerings, First Fruits, Generosity and so forth.

CONCLUSION

Giving churches prosper when they focus on reaching souls and preaching Jesus more than preaching on prosperity.

One of the imbalances that happens in today's church culture is a focus on the prosperity message and wealth and not on the real issues like heaven and hell. It's true that God desires that His children prosper and be blessed; however the Bible also teaches that we should learn to be content in life. The Scriptures balance out very well when it comes to how we should live and what we preach.

With so many books and resources on steps to success and how to gain wealth, many Pastors have slipped into preaching only the benefits of the Kingdom and not the commitments.

In Acts 8:9-24 it talks about another type of leader, what I choose to call a 'Simon the Sorcerer Ministry.' In these few passages of scripture, we read how he used to boast how great he was, and how all the people high and low gave him attention. Simon was saved and baptised under Philip's leadership. Then we read of Peter and John's visit to Samaria, where they prayed for new believers who were then baptised in the Holy Spirit. Simon asked to buy that gift, so he could do what they (Peter and John) did. Peter and John saw his heart and rebuked him sharply for wanting to use the Holy Spirit for personal gain.

Two lessons come out of this passage for me:

1. **We all need accountability in ministry.**

   Philip was a seasoned, qualified leader however, and he did not pick up on the heart of Simon the Sorcerer.

2. **We need to make sure our heart is always right before God.**

   Especially when it comes to money and glory! It is so easy to use the gift of God for personal fame and recognition and not to build His Church.

THE IMPORTANCE OF SMALL GROUPS

John 17:4 (NIV) – "I have brought you glory on earth by completing the work you gave me to do."

This is a statement by Jesus that should make us think. Let's ask ourselves, what exactly did Jesus finish? What was it that the Father had given Him to do?

- Had He evangelised the whole world? NO
- Had He healed all the people on the planet who were sick? NO
- Had He preached to and taught all the nations? NO
- Had He travelled throughout the world? NO
- Were all men saved? NO

I believe that what He finished was what the Father had assigned Him to do, He hadn't done *everything* as we may have imagined. As we study John 17:6-16 we understand that Jesus is addressing His disciples, especially the Twelve.

John 16:6-16 (NIV) - [6]"I have revealed you to those whom you gave me out of the world. They were yours; you gave them to me and they have obeyed your word. [7]Now they know that everything you have given me comes from you. [8]For I gave them the words you gave me and they accepted them. They knew with certainty that I came from you, and they believed that you sent me. [9]I pray for them. I am not praying for the world, but for those you have given me, for they are yours. [10]All I have is yours, and all you have is mine. And glory has come to me through them. [11]I will remain in the world no longer, but they are still in the world, and I am coming to you. Holy Father, protect them by the power of your name—the name you gave me—so that they may be one as we are one. ¹²While I was with them, I protected them and kept them safe by that name you gave me. None has been lost except the one doomed to destruction so that Scripture would be fulfilled. ¹³"I am coming to you now, but I say these things while I am still in the world, so that they may have the full measure of my joy within them. ¹⁴I have given them your word and the world has hated them, for they are not of the world any more than I am of the world. ¹⁵My prayer is not that you take them out of the world but that you protect them from the evil one. ¹⁶They are not of the world, even as I am not of it."

We see that Jesus invested more time in the Twelve.

We see that Jesus taught the greatest truths to the Twelve.

We see Jesus becoming more emotionally connected to the Twelve.

We see Jesus directing a special calling to the Twelve.

We see Jesus getting involved with the personal lives of the Twelve.

We see Jesus tied with a special friendship to the Twelve.

We see Jesus always taking with Him the Twelve.

We see Jesus investing His most precious time and most personal moments with the Twelve.

This is enough to cause us to understand that during the three and a half years of His ministry, His primary target was to prepare, teach and train this small group of twelve men so that they could continue His work.

Ephesians 4:11-13 (NIV) - ¹¹It was he who gave some to be apostles, some to be prophets, some to be evangelists, and some to be pastors and teachers, ¹²to prepare God's people for works of service, so that the body of Christ may be built up ¹³until we all reach unity in the faith and in the knowledge of the Son of God and become mature, attaining to the whole measure of the fullness of Christ.

These are scriptures we all know, as they refer to the five-fold ministry of the apostles, prophets, evangelists, teachers and Pastors. In the Ancient Greek text there is this phrase; "*kai autous tous edokes tous men...pros ton katartismon ton agion EIS ergon diakonias, EIS oikodomin tou somatos*" - Meaning, the work is not done by the apostles, prophets, evangelists, teachers and Pastors. These have the commission to prepare and to equip the people of God, so that the people do the work. This is the true image of the groups which are being trained; this is where we see the continuation of Jesus' strategy.

Proportionately, the time Jesus spent with the crowds in His public ministry was much less than the time He spent with the twelve. He did not give the deep truths, interpretations and revelations to the crowds, which He gave to the twelve. This strategy of Jesus must cause us to stop and think, is it possible that we have the wrong target? Jesus knew that the people had needs, but He chose to spend the greatest part of His ministry with His small group. Gather a few people around you to transform many lives.

Mark 3:13 (NIV) - Jesus went up on a mountainside and called to him those he wanted, and they came to him.

Jesus attracted the crowds, but He Himself chose true communication with a few, with His small group. It is often easy for us though, to choose and even to struggle to get big crowds. Jesus did not put the crowds and true, direct communion with His disciples, together in the same boat. His relationship with His disciples is the perfect example of relational interdependence. Many churches today promote a Christianity of signs and making an impression, and put very little emphasis on building strong interdependent relationships. However, being a follower of Jesus means following His example and living in fellowship with others and having strong relationships.

The Bible shows us that deep honest relationships, or true fellowship with others, offer four blessings:

- We receive **strength** when the storms of life hit.
- We gain **wisdom** from one another in order to take important decisions.
- We are **accountable** to one another and that brings spiritual increase.
- We find **acceptance** and that aids in the healing of wounds.

CELL GROUPS BRING INCREASE IN THE CHURCH

We all feel the need to belong somewhere. In a large crowd the individual is lost. As a member of a small group however, we feel like we belong somewhere, we are known, loved and feel cared for. No Pastor can manage alone to cover all the needs of the people. We have the well-known example of Moses when, on Mount Sinai, his father-in-law gave him a valuable piece of advice (Exodus 18).

Only in small groups can people be ministered to. When people feel that they are being cared for and that they belong, they begin to take part and become useful; they then feel healthy too. A healthy sheep will produce and reproduce. We are parts of a body and in order for that body to function; each member should be doing the job he has been called to do. As we ALL work together, God transforms the lives of the people. Within the small groups, each member can become the hand of God which will touch and change the lives of the other people.

THE BODY BECOMES FUNCTIONAL AND UNITED THROUGH THE GROUPS

Our society today has brought great loneliness to people and unfortunately the same loneliness exists in the churches too. Our bodies sit next to one another on the chairs of the church, but our souls are far apart. This situation must trouble us because the church is the family of God, this family must be a community built on authentic relationships. Spiritual increase will not exist in the church if it is not a healthy community with members who have fellowship with one another. Our souls should face one another in a true and deep relationship.

How can the church achieve something like this? Through the small groups meeting in homes, where they should take care to cultivate the following:

1. **To get to know the others and to allow them to get to know you.**
   Through the groups the others should get acquainted with us, both who we are and what our life is like. We want the people to care about us, to listen to us and to learn about what is troubling us. We also must be ready to listen to the others. To build a correct relationship and have true fellowship demands a love which is simple, authentic and true. This is the type of love we see in the Word of God. We should tear down the barriers which prevent healthy relationships. To know and become known, we need to leave aside our fear, embarrassment, pride and isolation and stop hiding in the crowd.

2. **To love and be loved in return.**

   John 15:13 (NIV) - Greater love has no one than this, that he lay down his life for his friends.

   Love requires learning to listen, to remember, to respect and especially to offer practical assistance. This is much easier in a small group. Within the group, we can function with an attitude of love.

3. **To serve and be served.**
   This requires humility. In order for us to allow someone to serve us, we first have to admit that we are in need and require ministry. When we serve someone (anyone, anytime, anywhere) we show the heart of Christ, but the best example of ministry is when we serve those in our own houses first, without expecting anything in return. True relationships are developed when people learn to love and serve one another.

4. **To check and be checked.**

    We are accountable to one another and our lives should be transparent when we live close to each other and have close relationships. This brings security because the others, who are close to me, see my mistakes and I see theirs. Admonition and monitoring saves lives. Our silence and our indifference can bring about disaster.

SMALL GROUPS PROVIDE GOOD PASTORING

John 10:11-15 (NIV) - [11]"I am the good shepherd. The good shepherd lays down his life for the sheep. [12]The hired hand is not the shepherd who owns the sheep. So when he sees the wolf coming, he abandons the sheep and runs away. Then the wolf attacks the flock and scatters it. [13]The man runs away because he is a hired hand and cares nothing for the sheep. [14]"I am the good shepherd; I know my sheep and my sheep know me— [15]just as the Father knows me and I know the Father—and I lay down my life for the sheep."

Jesus knew His sheep, but He wanted His sheep to know Him too. Without small groups, it is impossible for the sheep to be pastored. It is important for the Pastor both to know and to pastor his sheep. When we refer to 'pastoring' we mean:

1. **Care and Discipleship**

    Those who are wounded need support, prayer and encouragement. The same is true of families, those who are ill need company and prayer and the poor require provision. In addition, the people of God require discipleship so that they can reach the spiritual level that Christ has called them to reach. This is the only way that we can have balanced, healthy, happy believers.

2. **Immediate response to crisis**

    Many things happen in the lives of people, a crisis or unpleasant events hit suddenly. Within a group where the members have developed healthy relationships, people find comfort and they can assist and even find solutions to the problems of life (Galatians 6:2).

3. **Help in recovery and restoration**

    After every crisis, people need help in order to recover. For example, my group will pray for me and care for me after the sudden death of a person close to me. This will continue for some time, even when the other people around me continue with their own lives, my cell group remains close to me.

4. **Supporting one another**

The members of the groups learn how to give and receive spiritual help. It is important for the believers to learn to give and to minister, it is important for them to feel useful and to develop their gifts.

LEADERS OF THE SMALL GROUPS

Who to put in charge of the small groups is a very serious and fundamental consideration. The choice can bring blessing in the local church but also it can cause great upheaval. A good leader will lead the group into spiritual increase into ministry and to correct, healthy relationships.

Firstly you will have to find those leaders, so you are looking for people who:

1. Love God, the people and the Word of God and are faithful members of the church who have been tried and tested. Don't just look for people who are gifted. The person who loves God, the people, the Word and the local church is a potentially exceptional leader.

2. Listen for, search for and discover the reputation of that person. It must be a person you know and who the people of God have an opinion and witness for. The leaders do not descend from heaven but are birthed within the local body. If the person does not have a good reputation or report among the people, then do not promote them because they will not become good leaders.

Secondly, train those leaders. Every new leader must be given the right to fail or to make a mistake. At the same time they must know that the Pastor is beside them, supporting them. They also need to be trained in areas such as:

- Pastoring and service
- Problem solving
- How to arrange a Bible study
- Basic rules of communication
- How to gain the trust of their members

- How to deal with difficult people

Teach these leaders the spiritual DNA of your own ministry; communicate your own heart to them, the 'whys and wherefores' of the ministry.

Teach these leaders how wonderful it is for everyone to work together, not just in unity but wholly aligned to the goals of the church. We *all* aim together in the same direction.

They must also learn the fundamentals of the ministry of the church. It is essential that they know on which principles they must move and minister. For example: unity – obedience – availability – protective cover – responsibility – accountability – transparency – membership.

They must understand that everyone needs to speak the same language.

CONCLUSION

The example of Moses and the advice of his father-in-law is excellent (read Exodus 18:13-26).

The example of Jesus, and how we pay attention to the small group of twelve, is unsurpassable, unique.

Even worldly businesses use Biblical principles to advance. They delegate responsibilities to chosen people after having trained them and transferred to them the same spirit. Then there follows systematic, close monitoring. It seems that only the people of God have difficulty in understanding these things. We present a leadership which is fearful and centralized – maybe the time has come for us to change?

CHAPTER 11 – SIERD DE JONG

ACCOUNTABILITY AT ALL LEVELS

To many people, even to many Christians, accountability doesn't sound like a blessing. Accountability is seen to be similar to manipulation, control and oppression. In this chapter we are going to see what accountability is, why we need accountability and also look at the benefits of being accountable.

STRONG AND SAFE HOUSES NEED A GOOD ROOF

Returning again to the analogy of a house, we saw in Chapters 2 and 3 of this book that a house needs a good foundation in order to stand the floods. We also saw that a house needs a good structure to withstand the storms. But besides these things a house also needs a good roof to protect the house from the rain.

When we look again at the example of the tabernacle of Moses we see that the tabernacle of Moses had a good foundation, and that it had a solid structure. But the tabernacle of Moses also had a good roof. This roof was made out of several coverings including animal skins and fine linen, and it protected the inside of the house from things like rain, wind, dust and insects.

Just as the house of God in the Old Testament needed a good roof, so does the house of God in the New Testament, which is the church (1 Tim. 3:15).

WHAT IS ACCOUNTABILITY?

From the comparison that accountability is like a roof we can discover what accountability is.

1. Just as a roof protects the house, likewise accountability protects each of us.

    Accountability is not there to oppress and hinder us; indeed the opposite is true. It is to help us to become all that God wants us to be. Accountability keeps us from getting sidetracked and helps us to stay on course to fulfil our God-given destiny by living under the umbrella of God's protection and blessing.

2. As the roof of a house is something that is always over and above us, so has accountability to do with the authority that God has placed over us.

Just as a roof covers a house, so accountability functions as a spiritual covering for the believer in whom God dwells (1 Cor. 3:16), and who together with other believers form the house of God in a local church setting (Eph. 2:19-22; 1 Peter. 2:5).

Out of these two aspects, accountability can be defined as "To live under God's protection and blessing, through acknowledging, submitting to and obeying the authority that God has placed over us."

SPIRITUAL COVERING

Bearing in mind that accountability is like a covering, read the following passage of Scripture and notice the words "cover", "covered", "uncovered" or "covering" in relationship to accountability.

1 Corinthians 11:3-15 (NIV) - 3 'Now I want you to realize that the head of every man is Christ, and the head of the woman is man, and the head of Christ is God. 4 Every man who prays or prophesies with his head covered dishonours his head. 5 And every woman who prays or prophesies with her head uncovered dishonours her head — it is just as though her head were shaved. 6 If a woman does not cover her head, she should have her hair cut off; and if it is a disgrace for a woman to have her hair cut or shaved off, she should cover her head. 7 A man ought not to cover his head, since he is the image and glory of God; but the woman is the glory of man. 8 For man did not come from woman, but woman from man; 9 neither was man created for woman, but woman for man. 10 For this reason, and because of the angels, the woman ought

to have a sign of authority on her head. [11] In the Lord, however, woman is not independent of man, nor is man independent of woman. [12] For as woman came from man, so also man is born of woman. But everything comes from God. [13] Judge for yourselves: Is it proper for a woman to pray to God with her head uncovered? [14] Does not the very nature of things teach you that if a man has long hair, it is a disgrace to him, [15] but that if a woman has long hair, it is her glory? For long hair is given to her as a covering.'

This portion of scripture talks about order in the family, and the women in Corinth had to wear a head cover as a sign of accountability to their husbands. We are not going to look at the cultural aspects of wearing a head covering but at the spiritual lesson that can be drawn from it.

There are principles that apply to the natural family as well as to the Church and vice versa because the Church is the spiritual family of God (Eph. 3:15; Gal. 6:10). For example, as the man is the head of his wife, so is the Lord Jesus the Head of the Church (Eph. 1:22; Col. 1:18). As the Lord Jesus loved the Church by giving His life for her, likewise should a man love his wife (Eph. 5:25). And as the wife is to be under covering of her husband, so should every believer be under a spiritual covering of church authority (Eph. 5:23).

THE NEED FOR ACCOUNTABILITY

We read of the need for covering in 1 Corinthians 11 verse 10:

[10] 'For this reason, and because of the angels, the woman ought to have a sign of authority on her head.'

This is the key verse to understanding the need for accountability. It says "**because of the angels**". What has accountability to do with angels? When the Bible speaks about angels, it speaks about two groups of angels, of good angels and evil angels.

Satan started as a good angel, but fell and turned into an evil angel (Is. 14:12-15; Ez. 28:13-17). As an evil angel, Satan's main weapon is deception and one of Satan's main activities is to deceive people away from their commitment to God, from His plan and destiny for their lives (Gen. 3:1-4; Acts. 5:3; 2 Cor. 2:11; Eph. 6:11; 1 Tim. 2:14; John 8:44; 2 Thess. 2:9-10; Rev. 2:9, 24; 12:9; 13:14; 20:2-10).

The apostle Paul wrote:

2 Corinthians 11:2-4 (NIV) - [2] 'I am jealous for you with a godly jealousy. I promised you to one husband, to Christ, so that I might present you as a pure virgin to him. [3] But I am afraid that just as Eve was deceived by the serpent's cunning, your minds may somehow be led astray from your sincere and pure devotion to Christ. [4] For if someone comes to you and preaches a Jesus other than the Jesus we preached, or if you receive a different spirit from the one you received, or a different gospel from the one you accepted, you put up with it easily enough.'

In the book of Genesis we read how Eve was deceived. The serpent came to her with a suggestion that appealed to her pride - for her to be like God would make her independent of God. Instead of consulting Adam she acted on her own, and we know the rest of the story. She could have saved herself, and all who are affected by what she did, from this tragedy by having put herself under Adam's covering instead of independently acting on her own.

Eve, as the bride of Adam, is a type of the Church who is the bride of Christ (Rev. 21:9). All true believers belong to the bride of Christ. Just as Eve was vulnerable to deception, so are all believers. We are even more vulnerable than Eve was because we are born with a sinful nature, while Eve was deceived whilst in a sinless state.

Generally we can say that deception will try to make us believe and act upon a lie. But the way deception works is that the lie is wrapped up in truth, so it is not always easy to discern. That is why it is so deceiving. To rightly discern it you have to look deeper than just at the surface appearance, you have to think things through and not just jump to premature conclusions. There is a need for good judgement in order to come to right and wise conclusions, to save us and our churches from being unnecessarily damaged and hurt. This is especially true as the coming of the Lord is drawing near. The Bible states that in the last days there will be great deception (2 Thess. 2:9-12; Mark 13:22).

We must be aware that Satan plans to oppose the work that God wants to do through His Church and he therefore plans strategies to hinder, stop and destroy Christians and churches. The apostle Paul wrote:

2 Corinthians 2:11 (NKJV) - [11] 'lest Satan should take advantage of us; for we are not ignorant of his devices.'

The Greek word that is translated in the New King James Bible as "*devices*" is "*noema*". This word means:

- A mental perception, thought.
- An evil purpose.
- That which thinks, the mind, thoughts or purposes.

Satan thinks about what the best strategy is to hinder, and eventually stop, the Church in advancing in fulfilling God's purposes.

In the same way that Satan came to Eve with a suggestion that deceived her, making her believe that it would be for her benefit, so there are many things today that come our way that also try to get our attention. These suggestions may imply that we need something new to make us happy and successful. Church leaders also are faced with all kinds of new trends and moves that promise revival and church growth. These issues require good judgement because they are not always what they seem to be at first sight. They may seem to be a quick fix for the lack of church growth, but can be very damaging in the long term.

To have good judgement on every matter is not always easy and we do not have that kind of wisdom on our own. On our own we can be convinced that something is the right thing to do, but in the end it can turn out to be terribly wrong. The Bible says:

Proverbs 14:12 (New King James Version) - 'There is a way that seems right to a man, but its end is the way of death.'

The consequences of our bad judgements can be harmless, but they can also be painful or even fatal. That is one of the reasons why we need covering. We need covering in order to protect us from making painful, and even more importantly, fatal mistakes.

An example of this is taken from John Bevere's book *Honor's Reward*, pages 107-108. He tells this story:

> "Years ago the church went through a transition of leadership. She and her husband travelled a good distance to attend, so it seemed a good time to try other churches closer to their home. After visiting several, she liked a small church close to their neighbourhood. However, the husband felt it wasn't the place they should join; his

feeling was they should return to their original church. She did so reluctantly, but continued to go to the small church Sunday evenings.

She became more attached to and involved with the small church. Eventually the leaders of the smaller church challenged her, "When are you going to stand up to your husband and tell him you have to obey God's leading to come to our church?" Their words swayed her. She told her husband of her decision to switch churches; then she made an appointment with the pastor of the original church to inform him that she would leave even though her husband would still attend. The night before the meeting she got hold of my (that is John Bevere) book *Under Cover*, in which I (John Bevere) discuss the importance of submission to authority.

She said to me: "John, I stayed up the entire night reading it. I cried through the whole book; realizing my rebellion toward God and my husband. The following day I repented to both my husband and pastor."

She willingly returned to the church. After a few months the pastor's wife introduced her to a woman in the church. It turned out they both had a similar vision for a business venture, so they began the business. Today they are very successful and are putting a good amount of finances from their business into the kingdom of God.

She said: "John, had I stayed at the other church I would have eventually left my husband and never entered into the call of business that's on my life". She further shared that the small church whose leaders persuaded her to disregard her husband's leadership no longer existed. She honoured her husband, which resulted in both protection and reward".

She was saved from a lot of pain and disillusionment by her willingness to acknowledge the order God has placed in the home and by eventually submitting to her husband.

FOUR WAYS TO BE PROTECTED FROM DECEPTION

We are going to look briefly at four ways in which you can protect yourself from deception:

1. Decide to make the Word of God the highest authority in your life and surrender your will to His will unconditionally.

Psalm 119:1-8 (NIV) - [1] 'Blessed are they whose ways are blameless, who walk according to the law of the LORD. [2] Blessed are they who keep his statutes and seek him with all their heart. [3] They do nothing wrong; they walk in His ways. [4] You have laid down precepts that are to be fully obeyed. [5] Oh, that my ways were steadfast in obeying Your decrees! [6] Then I would not be put to shame when I consider all your commands. [7] I will praise You with an upright heart as I learn your righteous laws. [8] I will obey your decrees; do not utterly forsake me.'

By making God's word the highest authority in our life, and by surrendering our will to God's will unconditionally, God Himself will become our covering and our protection (Ps. 91).

2. Stay in the house where God has planted you.

Psalm 92:13 (NKJV) - 'Those who are planted in the house of the LORD shall flourish in the courts of our God.'

Our safety is our local church, because it is there where we are under covering. By staying in the house where God has planted us we stay under the authority that God has placed over us.

Brother Kevin Conner explains in one of his studies that on the Passover night, when the people of Israel in Egypt slew the lamb and applied the blood to their doorposts, all the Israelites were told to stay in their houses. It was in their houses that they were safe from the death-angel. What would have happened if some of the firstborn had left their houses that night? They would have been slain by the death-angel. Why would this have happened? It would have been because they were not under covering in a house that had blood on the doorposts.

Likewise it is important for all believers to be in the Church, which is the house of God (1 Tim. 3:15), that has been purchased with the blood of the Lord Jesus Christ (Acts 20:28). In the Church there is safety from deception because the Church is the pillar and foundation of truth (1 Tim. 3:15).

By not being under authority, you become a law unto yourself and you become more vulnerable to deception. By being under authority, you are under protection.

3.   Keep a love for the truth.

> John 8:32 (NKJV) - 'And you shall know the truth, and the truth shall make you free.'

We like this Scripture because it talks about being set free by the truth. But we must realise that before the truth sets us free it can make us feel miserable, because truth is not always pleasant to face. That is why we have the tendency to avoid being truthful with ourselves. It is easy to see the mistakes of our fellow brothers and sisters, and to criticize them for it, but it is hard to face the mistakes in our own lives. This is what Jesus meant when He said:

> Luke 6:41 (NKJV) - 'And why do you look at the speck in your brother's eye, but do not perceive the plank in your own eye?'

If we do not keep a love for the truth we will deceive ourselves and end up believing and acting upon a lie, and we will be led astray (Is. 53:6).

4.   Keep a humble spirit that is willing to receive instruction and correction.

> Proverbs 15:32-33 (NIV) - 32 'He who ignores discipline despises himself, but whoever heeds correction gains understanding. 33 The fear of the LORD teaches a man wisdom, and humility comes before honour.'

When someone is humble enough to be taught and to receive correction they will gain understanding and wisdom, and as a result of that they will experience promotion. So the process starts with humility and it ends with promotion. That's why the above scripture says: "*humility comes before honour.*" The Bible also says:

> James 4:10 (NKJV) - 'Humble yourselves in the sight of the Lord, and He will lift you up.'

> 1 Peter 5:5-6 (NKJV) - 5 '… and be clothed with humility, for "God resists the proud, but gives grace to the humble." 6 Therefore humble yourselves under the mighty hand of God, that He may exalt you in due time,'

ACCOUNTABILITY BUT NO CONTROL

In some Christian circles the principle of accountability has been abused and taken to extremes by the controlling of lives beyond the level that God ever intended. The shepherding movement is an example of this. Because Christians have been damaged by authority they react to it, and throw the baby away with the bathwater, by not wanting to be accountable to human authority. John Bevere in his book *Honor's Reward* page 101 writes:

> "We're to always honour and submit to authority; we're to obey authority as well; however in regard to obedience, we're not to obey an authority if they order us to do something contrary to the Word of God. An example may be if a parent tells a child to lie to their teacher, the child can respectfully say to their parent, "Mom or Dad, I respect and honour you, but I cannot lie, for that is a sin against God." Or a more severe case would be if a father is sexually assaulting a young person, the son or daughter is to seek help from other authorities. They do not dishonour their father by seeking to get him and themselves help."

A Biblical example is that of the apostles who were forbidden to preach in the name of Jesus by the Sanhedrin. Look at what Peter said:

Acts 5:29 (NIV) - 'Peter and the other apostles replied: "We must obey God rather than men!'

Not being able to obey because of Biblical reasons does not relieve us of our obligation to honour and submit to authority. John Bevere writes:"Obeying has to do with our actions, while submitting and honouring has to do with our attitude". David is the classic example of this. David could not obey Saul, but he still honoured and submitted to him as his anointed king and spiritual father.

1 Samuel 24:8 (NIV) - 'Then David went out of the cave and called out to Saul, "My lord the king!" When Saul looked behind him, David bowed down and prostrated himself with his face to the ground. 9 He said to Saul, "Why do you listen when men say, 'David is bent on harming you'? 10 This day you have seen with your own eyes how the LORD delivered you into my hands in the cave. Some urged me to kill you, but I spared you; I said, 'I will not lift my hand against my master, because he is the LORD's anointed.' 11 See, my father...'

We must always keep an attitude of submission and honour for our leaders. Peter says:

1 Peter 2:17 (Amplified) - 'Show respect for all men [treat them honourably]. Love the brotherhood (the Christian fraternity of which Christ is the Head). Reverence God. Honour the emperor.'

Peter wrote this letter between 63 and 65 AD. The emperor at that time was Nero, who ruled Rome from 54 to 68 AD. Emperors were generally harsh rulers who were not friendly towards Christians and this was especially true of Nero. Despite this Peter still tells Christians to keep an attitude of honour toward the emperor.

ACCOUNTABILITY AT ALL LEVELS

What about the leadership of a local church? Who is covering the leaders? A principle of leadership is that you lead by example (1 Cor. 11:1). A leader cannot ask something of the members that he is not willing to do himself. If the leaders ask the members of the church to be under covering of their leadership, whose covering are they under? Should there not be covering at all levels, including the senior leadership level also?

To answer this question of the accountability of church leaders we first must see the balance between the autonomy of the local church and the accountability of its leaders.

1. Autonomy

    The local church is like a family. As each family is to be an autonomous social unit, likewise should each local church be autonomous. Bill Scheidler explains in his book, *The New Testament Church and its Ministries*, that the autonomy of the local church means that it is self-governing, self-supporting and self-propagating. Let us look briefly at these three aspects.

    a. Self-governing

        I refer to Chapter 3 of this book, where it is explained in more detail how the local church is to be structured. Here it is enough to say that the Senior Pastor, with the elders, is under Christ, who is the Head of the Church. When a church has to answer to a headquarters it will undermine the autonomy of the church and the role of Christ as the Head of the Church.

    b. Self-supporting

        Just as a family has to be self supporting, so each local church has to be self-supporting. There may be a period when help from others is needed, but it should not be permanent. In Chapter 9 it is explained how a generous church can be cultivated in order to have more than enough, so that the church can support itself and bless others.

c. Self-propagating

As reproduction is normal to a natural family, so should it be normal to any local church as the family of God. That means growing in numbers, but also growing spiritually. It is the church's responsibility to go into the entire world and preach the gospel and it is also her responsibility to teach and raise believers up toward spiritual maturity.

2. Accountability

Although the local church is to be autonomous it is in the interest of the church and its leaders that the leaders of the church are accountable as well.

By being under authority one can exercise authority safely. Someone who is exercising authority without being under authority is potentially dangerous because there is no one who can speak into their life.

The elders are first of all accountable to the senior leader, and the senior leader should be walking in relationship with seasoned, trustworthy, God-ordained leaders to whom he is accountable. This brings great security to the church. The church members will feel safe with their leaders because they know that their leaders, to whom they are accountable, are also accountable themselves.

A church whose leaders are not under covering is a church without a spiritual roof. They are open to all kinds of issues that can come up and that are potentially destructive to the church. Besides that, to be a Pastor and not have someone to walk with in relationship as a Pastor, and to whom you can go for counsel, is a lonely and hard road to travel on one's own, and a road which many Pastors do not survive.

The Bible says that we as humans are in need of others (Eccl. 4:9-12; Gen. 2:18). Church leaders are just normal human beings who are also in need of a covering. This is not so that they can be controlled, but so that they can be protected, encouraged and blessed.

On a personal note my wife and I have found in MFE (Ministers Fellowship Europe) a great group of people where we feel safe and loved. Being part of MFE and walking in relationship with the Pastors and the leadership of MFE has encouraged us to continue in the ministry and not to give up. MFE has taught us principles that make church life great and we as Pastors and as a church would not be what we are today without the support of MFE. It is with the leadership of MFE where our accountability lies and we can recommend any Pastor in Europe to join this great group of leaders if they have not found anybody to walk with in the ministry.

COVERING RELEASES GOD'S ANOINTING

Covering is not just to protect us from negative things like deception, making bad judgements and being hurt but it also releases God's anointing upon our lives and churches. Psalm 133 says:

Psalm 133 (Amplified) - [1] 'Behold how good and pleasant it is for brethren to dwell together in unity! [2] It is like the precious ointment poured on the head, that ran down on the beard, even the beard of Aaron [the first high priest], that came down upon the collar and skirts of his garments [consecrating the whole body]. [3] It is like the dew of [lofty] Mount Hermon and the dew that comes on the hills of Zion; for there the Lord has commanded the blessing, even life forevermore [upon the high and the lowly].'

Verse 1 of this Psalm talks about how good it is to be in unity. First of all, you cannot have unity when there is no acknowledgment of authority. For example, can you image what it would be like if citizens did not submit to, and obey, the traffic laws? What chaos, anger and damage this would cause. Or can you image a family where the kids do not have to submit to and obey their parents? There would be disunity and fighting. What would happen in a church where the members do whatever they think is right? Authority is one of the ingredients that cause unity.

In the Trinity there is unity because there is an acceptance of order. One of the reasons why the Lord Jesus was so successful in His earthly ministry was because He was in submission and obedience to the Father (John 5:19), and in unity with the Father (John 17:20-24). By being in submission and obedience to the Father and in unity with the Father, the Lord Jesus positioned Himself to be anointed by the Father and succeed in His ministry (Luke 3:22; 4:18-19).

Being in submission and in unity with the covering God has placed over our lives, we position ourselves to be increasingly empowered to do the work God has called us to do. Look at what Psalm 133 continues to say:

"It is like the precious ointment poured on the head, that ran down on the beard, even the beard of Aaron [the first high priest], that came down upon the collar and skirts of his garments [consecrating the whole body]".

It flows from the head of the high priest down onto the body of the high priest. It flows from top to bottom. The anointing that is on the head that is above the body flows on the body that is under the head. This is a Godly principle. When we are under the covering and in unity with the leaders God has placed over us, the anointing, the success and the blessing that is on them will also come on us. The authority that is on them will also come on us, and we will be more effective in our ministries.

CONCLUSION

When we see all the good that comes out of being accountable, we can see that accountability is not something to be avoided, to run away from or to feel threatened by. It is something to be embraced because it protects us, it releases God's favour and His anointing, and it will cause each of us as individuals and the Church as a body to prosper, advance, and make a mark for God.

COVENANT RELATIONSHIPS

Covenant relationship is a subject that most people would say they understand and yet by their actions it is clear they don't. Not that it's a complicated subject, because it isn't; in fact it's quite straightforward. It's also a subject that can have a profound effect on the local church. Speaking purely for myself, I love the local church. Maybe this is because my experience of it has been so positive, but I value it, I appreciate its importance and really it's my extended family.

As for its importance, I would have to say that the local church is the main vehicle, or it should be, by which the Kingdom of God is established and extended. This is its purpose, which is why it's so important. Of course, what we have to appreciate is that the whole concept of local church was not designed by man, but by God, and it was designed to be successful in fulfilling its purpose.

Many churches fail to fulfil their purpose because of one particular thing and that is a lack of strong relationships. It doesn't matter that people adhere to the same Biblical doctrine, or that the church has great facilities and a great programme: all that keeps people together over the long term are the relationships that they have with one another. Even anointed ministry and the manifested presence of God won't stop people leaving our churches, which is staggering, but then we see this in the ministry of Jesus. When Jesus performed the miraculous, He attracted a huge crowd and they followed Him everywhere and yet as soon as He began to teach the things of the Kingdom, the vast majority left Him.

John 6:60 & 66 (NIV) "On hearing it, many disciples said, "This is hard teaching, who can accept it? ... From this time many of his disciples turned back and no longer followed Him."

Of course the local church should possess all these ingredients. It needs a programme that enables its people to actively participate. It needs its people to more or less be in one accord with their beliefs. Good facilities aren't essential but they are helpful and without a measure of anointing and the presence of God, there is not much point in gathering together in the first place. The thing is none of these ingredients stop people leaving, and stopping people leaving is important for a number of reasons - not least of which is that the less people we lose, the bigger our churches become. I am a great believer in big churches (relative to the size of the local community) because with greater size comes greater influence and every single church should aspire to be influential in its community.

Covenant is only one aspect of relationships but it is so important both for us as individuals and for our churches corporately. I want to start by considering the act of marriage, which is the obvious expression of a covenant relationship. Certainly in our culture, marriage is something that is entered into by two people who are already in a relationship and who want to commit themselves to each other - not just take their relationship to a deeper level which they could do by living together. That is why the marriage certificate is so important; it's a statement of commitment. Whatever culture applies, marriage begins with some kind of ceremony, an event that marks the beginning of this new stage in the relationship. In our culture this ceremony includes the making of promises and the exchanging of rings, the ring being a token of the covenant. Then, as we all know, this commitment to each other involves faithfulness and sacrifice.

A study of scripture shows that God wants us, as individuals, men with men and women with women, to have relationships with each other governed by the same principles as marriage.

> 1 Samuel 18:1-4 (NIV) - "After David had finished talking with Saul, Jonathan became one in spirit with David, and he loved him as himself. From that day Saul kept David with him and did not let him return to his father's house. And Jonathan made a covenant with David because he loved him as himself. Jonathan took off the robe he was wearing and gave it to David, along with his tunic, and even his sword, his bow and his belt."

What we have to understand is that David and Jonathan already had a relationship with each other which grew to the point that they wanted to do something that would guarantee that their relationship would last. So they made a covenant, it was an event, something to look back on and identify as the start of this new stage in their relationship. Their covenant wasn't assumed. Some people take as evidence of covenant the length of time a relationship has lasted, but longevity of relationship is not evidence of covenant. That's like comparing people who live together with people who are married. Marriage is a covenant, living together isn't. Neither is the intimacy of a relationship evidence of covenant because intimacy will not guarantee that a relationship will last. I imagine we can all look back over our lives and think of people we were once close to but with whom we are no longer in relationship. Covenant is the only means by which we can guarantee a relationship will last.

We see as well in this covenant that David and Jonathan made, that Jonathan gave David his robe, tunic, sword, bow and belt. In other words, Jonathan was giving David something to remind David of the covenant they had just made. These were the tokens of the covenant.

1 Samuel 20:12-17(NIV) - "Then Jonathan said to David: "By the LORD, the God of Israel, I will surely sound out my father by this time the day after tomorrow! If he is favourably disposed toward you, will I not send you word and let you know? But if my father is inclined to harm you, may the LORD deal with me, be it ever so severely, if I do not let you know and send you away safely. May the LORD be with you as he has been with my father? But show me unfailing kindness like that of the LORD as long as I live, so that I may not be killed, and do not ever cut off your kindness from my family—not even when the LORD has cut off every one of David's enemies from the face of the earth."

So Jonathan made a covenant with the house of David, saying, "May the LORD call David's enemies to account." And Jonathan had David reaffirm his oath out of love for him, because he loved him as he loved himself."

There we see, as in marriage, the ingredients of sacrifice and faithfulness. Sacrifice in that when Jonathan took David's side against Saul, he relinquished his right as the heir to the throne. In other words, he sacrificed his birthright. David, on the other hand, promised to look after Jonathan's family and we see David being faithful in this as he took in, as his own son, Jonathan's son Mephibosheth (2 Samuel 9:1-13). This actually is a wonderful expression of faithfulness in that Jonathan was already dead which would have given David the perfect opportunity to walk away from his promise. In fact custom dictated that, given the circumstances, David should have had all Saul's relatives killed, including Mephibosheth. Not only did he not kill Mephibosheth, but David took him in and treated him as his son.

When God created us, we were created as relational beings and our capacity for relationship exceeds what we get from marriage. As a man I need someone who truly understands what it is to be a man. A woman doesn't understand, not fully; how can she? She is not a man. A man doesn't understand what it's like to be a woman. I've been married twenty-nine years and I know my wife intimately, but even after all these years she will still react to some things that catch me totally by surprise. I am not saying that life is not worth living if we do not have the kind of relationships I am alluding to. Personally I could quite happily survive on the relationships I have with my wife and my sons, but the depth of these other relationships, what they do is enrich our lives. As a man I need someone other than my wife whom I can laugh with. This is relatively easy to achieve but if that's the depth of the relationship, whilst it's fun, it's nevertheless superficial. I also need someone, again other than my wife, who I can share my thoughts with and share my heart with and that's not so easy. To share your heart with someone is to make yourself vulnerable and that's risky and that's why we don't have many relationships of that depth. But I would go further and say that as a man I need someone, other men, who I can cry with and whilst that's rare, because it entails exposing yourself emotionally, where that depth of relationship exists there is true relational fulfilment.

My suggestion, therefore, is that if we have a relationship with someone and we want it to last for a lifetime, then make a covenant, but in doing so be aware that covenant is a serious business because it's done before God. Over the years I have known people make covenant, and some of these have been leaders of maturity and of some seniority, and yet for whatever reason the relationship just peters out. In a way, it's like they have entered into a conditional covenant. In other words "the covenant is conditional on me continuing to receive benefit from you", or "it's conditional on me being around" or "it's conditional on you not offending me". I repeat, covenant making is a serious business and Genesis 15:9-18 (NIV) emphasises this:

> 9-10 "So the LORD said to him, "Bring me a heifer, a goat and a ram, each three years old, along with a dove and a young pigeon." Abram brought all these to him, cut them in two and arranged the halves opposite each other."

> 12 "As the sun was setting, Abram fell into a deep sleep, and a thick and dreadful darkness came over him."

> 17-18 "When the sun had set and darkness had fallen, a smoking brazier with a blazing torch appeared and passed between the pieces. On that day the LORD made a covenant with Abram."

The imagery here is that if covenant is broken, then the blood that was spilled when the covenant was made would be on the hands of the covenant breaker, which of course is why we shouldn't make covenant with someone we do not really know. Of course, when we do make covenant, like marriage, it's supposed to last for a lifetime.

If we accept that covenant shouldn't be assumed, how then do we make covenant? Well, there is no set procedure as long as it's understood that there should be some kind of event to mark the beginning of this new stage in the relationship. By way of example, in my own case, when I first came across this principle I made covenants with two of my friends. I sent the first one a letter and in it I wrote that I would let him down, but when I did, it would never be intentionally. I also wrote that when he let me down - when, not if - I would never walk away from him. Over the years we have let each other down, but the relationship has been maintained because of the existence of a covenant, made before God, the evidence of which is a letter. With the second guy, because I wanted to give him some kind of token but wasn't sure he would understand what I was trying to do, I gave him something really stupid. In fact I gave him a used toothbrush! The reason being if he didn't understand, I could pass it off as a joke and hopefully retain some dignity. Let's not forget this principle was new to me and I was just "feeling my way". The thing is, after all these years I know he still has it and I know he values it because it's tangible evidence that he's got at least one friend whose loyalty he can count on, whatever the circumstances.

For covenant to work there has to be *loyalty*. The problem with loyalty is that we don't know how loyal we are until we are tested. Another problem is that everyone assumes they are loyal and yet the Bible says:

Proverbs 20:6 (Good News) - "Everyone talks about how loyal and faithful he is, but just try and find someone who really is."

You see, loyalty is maintaining relationship in the face of relational upset. Being hurt by someone, being let down by a friend, being offended by them, these are not acceptable reasons to break relationship. None of us is perfect and we would think it unreasonable if people expected perfection from us, and yet when someone displays their imperfection we often react in a totally unacceptable way.

1 Peter 4:8 (NIV) - "Love covers a multitude of sins."

In other words, make provision for someone else's failure. Make allowance for their imperfection, as we would hope they would make allowance for ours. Loyalty is indeed seeing the plank of wood in our eye and not the speck of dust in our brother's eye. Why should our friendships fail because of a display of imperfection when our marriages don't? The answer to that, at least in part, is that our marriage relationship has been formalised which helps keep it together. If we formalised our friendships wouldn't that have the same effect?

Besides loyalty, covenant requires *risk*. It's a risky business making a covenant promise before God that you are going to stick together come what may. Covenant also requires *effort*. Physical effort in making sure you find the time for each other and emotional effort in keeping the relationship going when you hit relational difficulties. It also requires *transparency*. You cannot have a meaningful relationship of any intimacy unless you are prepared to be open and honest with each other. Over the years I have heard lots of talk about the need for transparency, especially within leadership teams, but often where people say it exists, it's just a delusion. That's because true transparency is really difficult because it's incredibly risky. You really make yourself vulnerable when you share your heart with someone and you can only do it safely when there is a degree of *trust*, which is the other necessary ingredient of covenant. Yes, we have to learn to trust each other but you can only really do that when you know the one you are in relationship with is *committed* to you. So covenant requires loyalty, risk, effort, transparency, trust and long-term commitment, which if you think about it also sums up marriage. Different relationship; but the same principles.

As I wrote earlier, I've seen people make covenant with each other but then something happens and the relationship deteriorates. Maybe there is a disagreement and the relationship falls apart. Maybe something gets in the way like a new job in a different part of the country. Or maybe one of them falls out with church and so they leave and find somewhere else to worship and the relationship just fizzles out. All of these are examples of breaking covenant. If we walked out on our husband or wife we would not expect God to bless us. So why is it any different when we walk away from our covenant brother or sister? The reality is that if we break covenant with our friend, we move out of the blessing of God which is why we shouldn't make covenant lightly, oblivious to the consequences.

You may be forgiven for asking, therefore, if entering into a covenant is such a serious business and the consequences of failing are so far reaching, is it worth the risk? Well the point is that it is supposed to guarantee that our treasured relationships last and it's these lasting relationships which bring so much relational fulfilment.

Covenant of course is not only important to us as individuals, it's also important for Church as a whole. There is an interesting scripture in 1 Corinthians 1:10:

"I appeal to you, brothers, in the name of our Lord Jesus Christ, that all of you agree with one another so that there may be no divisions among you and that you may be perfectly united in mind and thought."

Have you ever wondered how that is possible? How in any church - particularly a large one - can there be no divisions and perfect unity? Well, covenant is the answer.

COVENANT ON A LIMITED SCALE CAN MAINTAIN UNITY ON A WIDER SCALE

Covenant has to be on a limited scale because there aren't enough hours in the day to have that kind of relationship with everyone, but the effect is anything but limited.

An example of this would be that if I have covenant relationship with someone in church and then something happens to potentially cause me to leave church, maybe I've been offended in some way, then that gives me a problem because if I leave, that detrimentally affects my covenant relationship. Therefore the existence of covenant forces me to sort out my problems within the church instead of leaving and in that way the division or the dispute is dealt with.

Psalm 133:1 & 3 (NIV) - "How good and pleasant it is when brothers (and sisters) live together in unity! ... For there the LORD bestows his blessing, even life forevermore."

The King James Version says:

"For there the Lord commands his blessings"

It's like an inescapable law, a bit like gravity. Gravity is a natural law that we are all subject to and likewise there are spiritual laws that we are subject to, for example, sowing and reaping. Whatever we sow we reap and if we sow unity we reap God's blessing and this blessing is for us as individuals and also for the church collectively.

Unity will never exist unless we determine in our hearts to maintain good relationships with each other, irrespective of the difficulties. Now that is easier said than done because maintaining good relationships, especially over a long period of time, can be blood, sweat and tears. It has been my experience, however, that making the effort is worth every drop of blood, every bead of sweat and every single tear because in amongst it all and at the end of it, there is the blessing of God.

BUILDING WITH JOY OVER TRADITION

Man is a creature of habit; he gets used to situations then has difficulty in accepting change. One name which we use to define hypocrisy and tradition, as opposed to truth and life, is the name of the Pharisees. The name Pharisee means religion, type and ceremony, it also means 'law'. All these are in contrast to joy, purity and genuineness in close relationships.

WHO WERE THE PHARISEES?

This group began during the war of the Maccabees, a family of priests who loved God and His law and fought against the idolaters who were trying to infiltrate Israel. The Pharisees were, from the time of the Maccabees, a group which for about two hundred years lived with very high principles and separated themselves from idol worship. The name Pharisee means 'set apart.' Before the birth of Christ they were characterized as righteous; they had boldness and there were times when Pharisees died a martyr's death when standing for their faith.

However, as is true of every religious group, they also had their weaknesses. Their motive for what they did was not their love or passion for God; it was their pride. This pride stemmed from the idea that they were separate and unique; they had gained an attitude of arrogance. Even though they were part of the Hebrew community, their customs and dress kept them apart from their brothers; they considered themselves to be too holy to mix with the others. The enforcing of their laws upon the people brought not joy and blessing, but a burden which they could not bear, as Christ pointed out (Luke 11:46). The attitude of the Word of God is clear, as expressed by the

Apostle Paul in Romans 14:17: "For the kingdom of God is not a matter of eating and drinking, but of righteousness, peace and joy in the Holy Spirit."

HOW IMPORTANT IS JOY?

We cannot ignore the words of Christ in John 15:11, 17:13 and 16:24. The Lord wants His people to live and to build with joy in their lives. As He himself said, in this world we will have tribulation, but He has overcome the world. He gave us His own joy.

> Romans 14:17 - "For the kingdom of God is not a matter of eating and drinking, but of righteousness, peace and joy in the Holy Spirit."

As we are involved in the expansion of the Kingdom of God, we must ask ourselves what kind of kingdom are we expanding and what are its characteristics? Is it the kind that the Word of God presents so simply?

BUILDING LIKE THE PHARISEES, BASED ON RELIGION AND TRADITION

Our aim should be the expansion of the Kingdom as the Lord desires, which is through the Holy Spirit and not through the spirit of religion as determined by religious tradition. There are warning signs to discern this spirit when it infiltrates into our lives, and to recognize its tactics. Maybe we have even unwittingly used these same tactics ourselves. Let's test ourselves and see what applies to us:

Characteristics of people with a religious spirit who are clinging to tradition:

1. They consider their basic mission to be the elimination of anything they think is wrong. These people create division in the church.
2. They have an attitude of heart which says, "I don't listen to people, I only listen to God." So we remember the Pharisees' answer, "We have Abraham as our father, who are you?"
3. They tend to find mistakes in other people and churches, rather than finding what is good about them.
4. Their ministry lacks mercy and understanding towards those who have sinned or failed.
5. They boast about their own spiritual maturity and gifts and constantly compare themselves with others.

6. They do things simply to be seen by others, just like the Pharisees, who would pray and show mercy with pride and exhibition.

7. They are suspicious of every new movement, new church or generally anything new that God is doing in people's lives.

8. They overreact to new believers who, naturally, are immature and so act in an immature fashion.

9. They don't want to change any of their habits, nor do they want the routine spiritual functions of the church to change, they want things to go on as they always have done.

THE DAMAGE DONE BY TRADITION AND RELIGION

What Jesus taught his disciples in prayer is clear. In Matthew 6:10, He says, "Your kingdom come, your will be done on earth as it is in heaven." This kingdom will bring righteousness, peace and joy in the Holy Spirit (Romans 14:17).

Contrastingly, Satan tries to plant in the church whatever is counterfeit, a false copy, which is what 'religion' is, with its works and traditions. These are the weeds growing along with the grain in the field of the Lord and because they grow up beside the true grain and look similar to the principles of the gospel, we don't recognize them. Of course, Satan wants religion to look good.

This is how the truth of Christ is gradually turned into traditions and religion:

1. **We place too much emphasis on outward appearance**
   The fear of what other people will think is always present. We forget that our attitude of heart is what God is interested in and not outward appearance.

2. **There is an attitude of selfishness, pride and condemnation**
   The religious spirit will *always* condemn someone if they don't do things correctly. There is always a fear of failure. In the Kingdom of God there is *mercy* for those who are seeking to find God. David was guilty of many serious sins but he was also a man after God's own heart.

3. **There is legalism which oppresses**
   The religious spirit offers a system of laws and rules without any leeway. It tries to produce a *method* which will replace creative *relationships*. The religious spirit gives us the rules which we must follow, and assesses us by our ability to fulfil those rules.

4. **It overemphasizes human effort**

   In religion and tradition, righteousness and holiness are gained through an individual's hard work and effort. This spirit says to the people, "You failed because you didn't try hard enough." In the Kingdom of God, righteousness is gained through the Holy Spirit (Romans 8:4). Holiness comes through a living, true relationship with Jesus. The more we surrender ourselves to the Lord, the more Christ's character is formed in us.

The Great Failure of Religion and Tradition

Jesus' disciples, who were simple people, did things that enraged the Pharisees. They ate, for example, with unwashed hands which, according to the Pharisees, was a great sin. Unfortunately this was a tradition which, over the centuries, had become very powerful. It was oral tradition which had never been given by Moses in written form. These oral traditions became the doctrine of the Pharisees and such teachings still exist today in many religious groups. Jesus, on the other hand, attacks these strongly with His Word. He exposes the Pharisees, saying that they give greater value to their traditions than they do to the living Word of God (Matt.15:6). This attitude, this tragic mistake, removes the authority from the Word of God in people's lives. The result is a lack of life. Religion and traditions lead us to spiritual bankruptcy.

The tragic consequences of this bankruptcy are:

1. We constantly seek for grace, victory and salvation, but unfortunately we never find them because the traditions of people cannot bring us joy and mercy in our lives.
2. We do works of righteousness but we never feel deep inside us the joy of God's acceptance (Romans 11:5-6).
3. During the services there is a feeling that there is something good in the atmosphere, but it is 'lost' when the service is over.
4. We go to church, but when we get back home we have become harder, more unbelieving than before.
5. We are permanently bound by fleshly desires and we know that we live in disobedience towards God but are unable to do anything about it.
6. God is, for us, someone who is waiting in the corner, hiding, he is waiting for us to make a mistake and catch us red-handed in order to punish us severely.

How Can We Protect Our Souls?

Jesus, in Luke 4:4, 8 & 12, gives us the perfect example of how to stand against the attacks of Satan. We face each attack with absolute trust in the character of God and His Word.

1. **Put the Lord first**

    The spiritual battle is all about who will gain our worship, is it God or Satan I wonder? Satan tricks us into putting people, circumstances, traditions and things before God. Protect yourself and the church by putting Christ above everyone and everything. Direct your worship towards Jesus, make this a basic, daily priority in your life. Don't replace worship with anything else; because our worship towards the face of the Lord stirs up passion inside us for our Lord, it also stirs up the love and joy that we encounter in His presence.

    If the Lord is first in your life, then it is certain that passion for Christ will be born and will increase inside you (Romans 12:10-11). Dead tradition and dead religion will extinguish our fire and passion for Jesus.

2. **Die daily**

    In order for Christ to have the first place in your life, you must die daily. Choose to die to anything that concerns the flesh, your plans, your emotions and your ways. After you have died, don't remain dead, but allow Christ to resurrect you and give you new life, His life. Choose His plans, His will, His aims and His desires. Protect your soul from the spirit of religion.

3. **Put on the armour**

    The spirit of religion prefers you to dress in the robes of bitterness, anger, condemnation, hatred, fanaticism, unforgiveness and division. But Jesus has designed other clothes for us; each piece of clothing represents something God wants to do in our lives and also through our lives.

    This universal clothing is:
    a. Jesus Christ (Romans 13:14).
    b. New life (Col. 3:10).
    c. A garment of praise (Isaiah 61:3).

    d.   Compassion, kindness, humility, gentleness and patience with love (Col.3:12 to 14).

    e.   Faith, love and the hope of salvation (1 Thess. 5:8).

    f.   The armour of light (Romans 13:12).

    g.   All the armour of God (Eph. 6:13-17).

4.   **Walk in truth**

The spirit of tradition and religion has distorted the truth of the Word. This has been done in such a way that it gives the impression that it is itself spiritual, but in reality it contrasts the Word. The spirit of tradition and religion uses scripture in isolation and out of context. In this way, it uses a part of the truth in order to deceive; it causes people to want to use the Word to hurt others. This is why it is necessary to know the Word of God, to know the heart of God and to know His character. Protect your soul, making the search for truth, walking in truth, speaking in truth and of course belief in truth, your priority.

CONCLUSION

The Lord has called us to walk in the fullness of the Holy Spirit. He has promised us life in abundance; He has not called us to misery, agony of soul, fear, religion or traditions. He has equipped us, and is equipping us, with His joy; this joy is the result of a deep personal relationship with Him.

1.   Honour God more than you honour people and traditions.

2.   Fear God and not man or what people might say about you. In this way you will not feel the need to do things just to please other people or so that you will look good in their eyes.

3.   Find time to stay in the presence of the Lord and sit at His feet, communicate with Him and enjoy Him.

4.   Search for the will of God and not man, find out what God really wants from you, what He is thinking and saying. Choose to live for your Saviour and not for traditions.

5.   Desire to carry out the instructions of the Lord and his commandments each day of your life.

If you carry out all of these, your life will be characterised by the joy of the Lord, a joy of the spirit written deep in the heart, which has nothing to do with feelings. This joy is the best material to build with, it attracts people, and it draws people closer to Jesus. The Church is readying herself for her marriage with the Lamb. All this preparation and the period of preparation is a period of joy and celebration. The spirit of the bride and the bridegroom is a spirit of joy. Let's come, therefore, to the throne of God with joy, singing hymns and praises and with a joyful sound.

Chapter 14 – Colin Cooper

Ingredients For Dynamic Worship

Worship – wow, what a subject! We were created to be worshippers by God himself; but what are the ingredients for dynamic worship in our churches? John 4:20-24 says the kind of worshippers the Father seeks are those who worship in spirit and in truth. So if there are true worshippers there must also be false worshippers, which is a sobering thought! Mark 7:6-9 - Jesus was answering some questions from the Pharisees – listen to what Jesus said, "People honour Me with their lips but their hearts are far from Me, they worship Me in vain and their teachings are rules from men which are pure traditions of their own".

What are traditions? The Oxford Modern English Dictionary puts it this way – "A custom or an opinion handed down". So often we do a form of worship which is not backed by Biblical principles or direction; so that's what it is – a *form* of worship. Somewhere in history, Biblical Worship was lost and was substituted by man's effort and ideas.

How did this happen? How did we get such a variety of different forms? I have heard many times from various groups and people that God is a God of variety and so there are many different expressions and ways to worship Him. But I have difficulty with that. In fact there is not the slightest hint or suggestion of it anywhere from Genesis to Revelation. However my thoughts are not to be the last word on anything. People's opinions, whether Biblical scholar or layman, must not be the last word on anything. The Word itself is to be the last word, not an isolated passage to make the Bible say what we want it to say, but allowing the whole of the Bible to balance out the whole of the Bible.

So where have the varied forms of what man has said is Worship (although the Word would say otherwise) come from? Well a very brief look at the history of the Church would help greatly.

Now we all understand from Scripture that Jesus gave Apostles, Prophets, Evangelists, Pastors and Teachers to the Church. It was not the Holy Spirit, but Jesus who gave these gifts to the Church, so that the body might be built up and might attain the whole measure of the fullness of Christ (Ephesians 4v11-13). Nowhere in Scripture do we read that He has taken them back.

So, *Church History* – let's take a brief look. In New Testament times the Church achieved a measure of supernatural power as the Apostles preached the Word and laid the foundations of the Church. A great book on Apostles is one written by Bill Scheidler called *Apostles: The Fathering Servant*. However, the New Testament Church had a period of decline – here's a quick look at the period:

100AD	Apostles no longer functioned, so good church foundations became weak.
130AD	Praying and putting hands on people simply became a ritual by priests.
135AD	The gifting of the Prophet was no longer used and, with the seer, the Church got itself into trouble.
155AD	The gifts of the Spirit no longer functioned in the Church – without these the Church became dry and ritualistic.
165AD	Plurality of leadership was replaced by one-man churches where the Priest, Minister or Pastor did everything.
190AD	An unscriptural practice of baptising babies, rather than adults repenting and being Baptised, came into the Church (Acts 2:38-39).
200AD	Liturgy in worship and ritual became normal - in other words it was form, not Spirit.
225AD	Church membership was given when people accepted the creed rather than "Believe in the Lord Jesus Christ and you will be saved" (Rom 10:9). Also people never heard about Christians being Priests and Kings (1 Peter 2:5 & 9).
350AD	The Emperor Constantine embraced Christianity but having little teaching or understanding, he compelled the heathen and pagans to adopt Christian practices. Thus the Church had a high proportion of non-Christians functioning in it, and with them came pagan rituals and practices which we still have today.
360AD	Rome became the absolute authority over the Church.
400AD	This was a dark time for the Church and history called it the "Church in the Dark Ages".

So the Church and how worship was organised was a pale shadow of the original New Testament Church. But hold on just a minute, Ephesians 5:27 says, "Christ will present the Church to Himself – radiant, no stain or blemish, holy, blameless". Now we are clearly not even remotely like this; if you're not sure, look at the person sitting next to you on Sunday!

But the early disciples understood something and had a glimpse of the future. Turn to Acts 15:15-18. "David's fallen tent, its ruins I will rebuild and restore", verse 18 says, "these things have been known for ages", and in verse 15 the disciples were very excited because they said, "the prophets are in agreement with this." Now after this statement we have to look at what the prophets have said – so let's look at Amos 9:11-12 – recognise it? This is what the disciples were excited about as this scripture now comes through the cross. The apostles (who were church planters) were ecstatic, as the Lord's promise to restore His Church became a reality.

So here we are with the Church in the Dark Ages – how do we translate all of this into real life? Remember what the Church will be like in the end before Jesus returns? Radiant, no stain or blemish, holy, blameless (Ephesians 5:27). So God looked on the Church in the Dark Ages and blew supernaturally to begin a process of restoring His Church. This is the sequence of events:

1517AD	God revealed that there was justification by faith in Jesus to a man called Martin Luther in Germany. At the time, people repented from sin by paying money to the priests. This practice was called indulgence. Martin Luther preached that the forgiveness of sins can only come through the saving grace of Jesus, and so through him God restored justification by faith in Jesus.
1520AD	God moved supernaturally through people who saw that it was not just faith in Jesus that was needed, but that the Bible said "Repent and be baptised for the forgiveness of sin" (Acts 2:38). This group preached repentance and water baptism. Some of the Lutherans thought that they were heretics and offered to baptise them, but then held them under the water long enough to drown them. As in this case, men can focus so intently on what God did yesterday that they miss what He is doing today. The people that preached repentance and water baptism were called the Anabaptists and it is from this that the modern Baptist Movement derives its name.
1700AD	This year saw the Moravian Movement, which introduced praying back into the Church. Also the Pentecostal Holiness Movement came about – God was restoring, bit by bit, lost truth back into His Church.

1750AD   John Wesley also started to preach holiness and sanctification in a church in Leicester, England. He cast one hundred people out of the church - because they did not have enough zeal for the Lord! This zeal was evident in both John and also his brother Charles; this led to the birth of the Methodist Chapel, and Charles wrote over one thousand hymns, many of which are still sung today.

1800AD   J.N Darby and others were seeking God and they had a revelation as God once again blew His breath on the earth. The revelation was that Jesus Christ would return once more to the earth. They left the established church and a movement started called the Brethren. They established what today we call Bible Studies so people could be instructed in the truth.

1900AD   God again blew His Spirit out and for the first time in almost two thousand years; people from all denominations were baptised in the Holy Spirit and spoke in "Tongues" (Acts 2:4). The established church did not accept this phenomenon so those who were baptised in this Spirit left, and the Pentecostal movement began.

1906AD   In a street called Azusa in Los Angeles, USA, the Holy Spirit was poured out and people began to use Gifts of the Spirit and Ministry Gifts. The Church was gathering pace. A black Baptist Minister called Brother Seymour seemed to be the prominent individual here.

1948AD   Hey, this was the year I was born! Something called the Canadian revival took place. This was the first time that spontaneous praise broke out in a large-scale gathering. Spontaneous worship, Spiritual songs and the laying on of hands – Biblical worship was being restored to the Lord's Church.

1965AD   Other denominations began to experience what the Pentecostals had gone through - Baptism in the Spirit and speaking in Tongues. Praise and Worship and Prophecy began again, and just like the Pentecostals, people experiencing this met hostility in their denominations. Gradually they left and a new movement began called the 'Charismatics'. God was pouring His Spirit out on others and not just the Pentecostals. The Prophet Joel spoke of this in Joel 2:28-29.

1973AD   Amos 9:11-12, Acts 15:15-18. The restoration of the Church was preached in various parts of the world by men who had not met or heard about each other, and like every move it was ridiculed by those who were stuck in God's move of previous years. Those who preached this message were known as restorationists and many Pentecostals and Charismatics rejected them, so they left these groups and started their own churches. They were given the name of 'House Churches' because on leaving the denomination they began to meet in homes. Others were called 'Restoration Churches'.

So God restored, little by little, truth that had been lost to the Church. But why did God not just do it all at once? That's what I would have done right back there with Luther - it would have saved a lot of time! Well, God did not because one little truth restored was met with ridicule by good people. So if it was all restored at once it would have killed us all off. We could not have handled it. But we still have some way to go before the Church is without blemish or stain.

Some of the promises that God will restore are the following:

1. The establishment of the House of the Lord - Isaiah 2:2.
2. The Tabernacle of David (Worship) - Amos 9:11, Acts 15:15.
3. Outpouring of the Holy Spirit - Joel 2:28-29.
4. Voice of the Bridegroom - Rev 19:7.
5. The glory of the Lord restored - 2 Chronicles 5:11.
6. Wise shepherding and wise judges - Isaiah 1:26.
7. Teachers of the Word - Isaiah 30:19-21.
8. Family relationships - Malachi 4:5.
9. Healing and health - 1 Kings 17:22, John 14:12.
10. Salvation of the unconverted - Matt 13:47-49.

So over the years many things have been, and in the future will be, restored to the Church. Now we have a glimpse as to how we have had 'form' in the Church, and why worship was a form in the Lord's house. The Almighty has begun to restore true worship and this is what we will now look at from a Biblical perspective.

For many of us, we were converted into worship where we would stand for a hymn, sit down for prayer, another hymn, then a prayer – it was called a 'Hymn prayer sandwich'. But in 1948, spontaneous praise and worship broke out and in the 1970s and 1980s this was accelerated across the world. In Biblical terminology it was named 'Davidic Worship'. Why?

Remember Amos 9:11-12 and Acts 15:15 "I will restore David's fallen tent and rebuild it as it used to be". Did this mean a literal tent or tabernacle would be built again? Of course not – we have to remember that the Old Testament is a shadow of The New Testament, so we have to bring it through the cross. David's tent had 3 parts to it – The Outer Court, The Inner Court and The Holy of Holies. Now this is just a quick panoramic view, not an in depth study, but it is a scriptural principle given to help us understand worship. The Outer Court is where the priest would enter. He would wash himself in the Laver, as God had instructed Moses not to let Aaron enter unless he first cleansed himself (Leviticus 16:2). Having done that he would proceed to the Inner Court which was lit by oil lamps and candles – in other words artificial light. After the Inner Court he would proceed to the Holy of Holies. In there was the Ark of God and no artificial light; it was lit by the pure light of God Himself, lit by His glory where His pure undiluted light would cast no shadows. It would be lit like Heaven is lit. Now let's bring this through the cross.

Scripture tells us that we as humans have three parts to us: 1 Thessalonians 5:23 - body, soul and spirit – as we are built in the Lord's image – the three parts being, Father, Son and Spirit. Our bodies are like the Outer Courts of the tabernacle. As the priest would cleanse himself so he would not die, so should we before entering worship. Exodus 30:20 - if we operated like this most of us today would be dead – thank God for the cross! But we need to be clean before worship because the principle still stands. How do we clean ourselves? In the church that I am based in, we have 15 - 20 minutes of prayer before the service, which we call 'Pre-wash'. The purpose is to ask the Lord to take the cares of the week away and make requests for Him to come and anoint the musicians, congregation, preacher and anything else for that meeting – in effect preparing ourselves for worship. We ask all who are taking part in the service to be there. Then we begin. So how do we begin? Again what does scripture say?

Let's look at Psalm 100:4 which says, "Enter His gates with thanksgiving and His courts with praise, give thanks to Him and praise His name". Our body is the Outer Court, so we clap, sing and dance (Psalm 47:1 "Clap your hands all the nations") as we go through the Outer Courts as priests and Kings.

Rev 1:5-6, 1 Peter 2:9 - A royal priesthood, Heb 2:12 - "I will declare your glory and sing praises in the presence of the people". It's not waiting for the Spirit to move me to clap, dance etc but an act of my will. This is, with our lips, a part of the Outer Court (1 Chronicles 16:29 "ascribe to the Lord the glory due to His name"). Over and over throughout the Bible it talks about clapping, dancing, shouting and praising, so this is the first part of a normal congregational gathering in the Bible.

The second part was entering from the outer courts into the Holy place. The Holy place in our bodies is the soul, the part of the emotions and thinking. It's where we feel. The Lord created our emotions, and when I tell the Lord that I love Him I can sometimes be overwhelmed by His love and cry with emotion – what a wonderful time to be near the Lord. At this point most churches would halt the service and go no further, but remember we have yet to enter the third part of the tabernacle – The Holy of Holies. We have been in the Outer Courts and progressed into the Holy

Place but we are not worshipping in the Spirit. As we press on, we begin to enter the Holy of Holies, the place where the presence of the Lord dwells. In fact, the Bible tells us what can happen in this place, so turn to 2 Chronicles 5. In verse 11 it says, "All the priests consecrated themselves". That's a good start; now verse 12 says "There were trumpets, singers in unison, cymbals and other instruments" then...then...then..., "The temple was filled with a cloud and the priests could not perform their service because of the cloud, for the glory of the Lord filled the temple". Wow! If only Sunday morning church was like this! But having said that, the Bible indicates that with the right ingredients church *can* be like this! So church is the outworking of the temple in the Old Testament and right now God is restoring His Church.

OUTER COURT / INNER COURT / HOLY OF HOLIES
BODY   SOUL   SPIRIT

Above is a simple illustration of the layout of the tabernacle. Some churches try to start with immediate worship, or jump into the Holy of Holies first. Some try and jump from the Outer Court to the Holy of Holies. Others start with the Inner Court, go back to the Outer Court, then to the Holy of Holies – but it is impossible to start with worship then go to praise, then put our requests in the middle and worship again.

No – first the cleansing of ourselves, getting rid of all the things that we have picked up during the week so we are clean vessels. Then we bring our praises. 1 Peter 2:5 – sacrifices acceptable to God. Cain brought fruit which was not acceptable (Genesis 4:3-7), but Abel brought meat and the Lord accepted his offering. Why? Well Cain brought fruit which was neat, clean and tidy, but God said a lamb was to be sacrificed, and blood was not as tidy as fruit! We are to bring only what is acceptable to the Lord – we cannot worship any way we like. So we follow the principles for worship which are in the Bible, God's Word. The Lord is seeking those who would worship in spirit and in truth. The principles for worship, which are clearly written in the Bible, give us access to dynamic worship, and in His presence come the miracles and the healings with other signs and wonders. So let's press in to Him; praise Him, love Him and live in His presence.

Chapter 15 – Sierd De Jong

The Importance of Prayer and Fasting

The regular practice of prayer and fasting is one of the major disciplines in which Christians and churches struggle. In this chapter we are going to look at the importance of prayer and fasting, and at how it functioned in the life of the Lord Jesus and also in the early Church, and how it is a vital part of church life today.

What is Prayer and What is Fasting?

1. **Prayer**

   Prayer is taking time to talk to God. This can be done by thanking Him and praising Him. It can be done by confessing our sins to God. It can also mean that we ask things from God for ourselves or for others such as our family, our church, or our city.

2. **Fasting**

   Fasting is to take a period where we abstain from eating or even sometimes from drinking. Eating and drinking are the basic needs that we have as human beings. Hunger and thirst are some of the strongest appetites a human being possesses: by fasting we acknowledge that we need God more than natural sustenance.

   Fasting can be done by the believer individually and also as a church corporately. It can be done in a general way to strengthen and deepen our personal relationship with God in order for God's purposes to be fulfilled in a greater measure. Later on in this chapter it will be explained how this functioned in the life of the Lord Jesus Christ. Fasting can also be done for specific purposes. Take for example Queen Esther. She called upon the Jewish people to fast for 3 days in order to save their lives, because of the plan that Haman had devised to destroy them (Esther 4:3,16). By doing this a great victory was won.

By adding fasting to our prayers, we express the seriousness of our desire to see God move in our lives or in a specific situation. It causes our prayers to be heard loud and clear in heaven (Is. 58:4).

FASTING IS NOT ONLY AN OLD TESTAMENT PRACTICE

Sometimes believers hold the misunderstanding that fasting was an Old Testament practice and that, because of the cross, it is of no benefit for New Covenant believers. However it is important to realise that not all Old Testament commandments and practices are done away with at the Cross. Take for example the commandment: "Thou shall not kill". That is an Old Testament commandment that still stands in the New Testament. This commandment is reinforced in the New Testament and even taken to a deeper level by the Lord Jesus (Matt. 5:21-26). Another example is the Old Testament commandment: "Thou shall not steal". This commandment is also repeated and reinforced in the New Testament.

Ephesians 4:28 (NIV) - He who has been stealing must steal no longer, but must work, doing something useful with his own hands, that he may have something to share with those in need.

The same is true for the practice of fasting. The Lord Jesus expected His disciples to fast when He had finished His work on earth and had ascended to heaven.

Matthew 9:14-15 (NIV) - 14 Then John's disciples came and asked him, "How is it that we and the Pharisees fast, but your disciples do not fast?" 15 Jesus answered, "How can the guests of the bridegroom mourn while he is with them? The time will come when the bridegroom will be taken from them; then they will fast.

In the next verse the Lord Jesus said:

Matthew 6:16 (NIV) - "When you fast, do not look sombre as the hypocrites do, for they disfigure their faces to show men they are fasting. I tell you the truth, they have received their reward in full.

Notice that the Lord Jesus did not say: "*If you fast*". No, He said, "*When you fast,*" Again, the Lord Jesus expected His disciples to fast after He had ascended into heaven and, in obedience to Christ's instructions, the early Church practiced fasting.

Not only was fasting practiced by the early Church it also was practised by the Lord Jesus Christ Himself, as we are going to see later on in this chapter.

When we take into consideration that the Lord Jesus fasted Himself, that He ordered and expected His disciples to fast after He had gone to heaven, and that the early Church practised fasting as well, then we can conclude that fasting is not just an Old Testament discipline that has been abolished at the cross, but that it should be practiced by New Testament believers even today.

PRAYER IN THE LIFE OF THE LORD JESUS

There are many scriptures that make it clear that the Lord Jesus was a man of prayer (Luke 3:21; 4:1-2; 5:16; 6:12; 9:18 etc). Through prayer the Lord Jesus saw the heavens opened and the Holy Spirit descending on Him to empower Him for His ministry.

Luke 3:21-22 (NIV) - [21] When all the people were being baptized, Jesus was baptized too. And as He was praying, heaven was opened [22] and the Holy Spirit descended on Him in bodily form like a dove. And a voice came from heaven: "You are my Son, whom I love; with you I am well pleased."

Prayer causes the heavens to open and the Holy Spirit to descend into our midst as it did in the life of the Lord Jesus. Prayer was a vital part of the life and ministry of the Lord Jesus. It had such an impact on His life and ministry that His prayer life was contagious. It made His disciples desire to be persons of prayer themselves. We can see that in the next scripture:

Luke 11:1 (NKJV) - Now it came to pass, as He was praying in a certain place, when He ceased, that one of His disciples said to Him, "Lord, teach us to pray, as John also taught his disciples."

The disciples had heard the Lord Jesus preach the greatest sermons; they had seen Him performing the greatest miracles. But we never read that they asked, "Lord, teach us to preach" or "Lord, teach us to perform miracles". No, instead they asked, *"Lord, teach us to pray"*. The disciples must have realised that all the other things were the result of the life of prayer that the Lord Jesus led. That created in them a desire to be persons of prayer as well.

FASTING IN THE LIFE OF THE LORD JESUS

Luke 4:1-2 (NKJV) - [1] Then Jesus, being filled with the Holy Spirit, returned from the Jordan and was led by the Spirit into the wilderness, [2] being tempted for forty days by the devil. And in those days He ate nothing, and afterward, when they had ended, He was hungry.

The first thing the Holy Spirit did after He had descended on the Lord Jesus in the form of a dove was to lead the Lord Jesus into the wilderness, where He fasted for 40 days. It was at the end of this time of prayer and fasting that Satan tempted the Lord Jesus, but the Lord Jesus overcame this temptation. Part of the reason He overcame was because He had prayed and fasted. It is strange that Christians and churches think that they do not need prayer and fasting to be an over-comer, while the Lord Jesus did. But there is more to fasting than overcoming. The next verses will show us that.

Luke 4:13-14 (NKJV) - [13] Now when the devil had ended every temptation, he departed from Him until an opportune time. [14] Then Jesus returned in the power of the Spirit to Galilee...

We read in Luke 4:1, "Jesus, *being filled with the Holy Spirit*." This was before the 40 days of prayer and fasting. After the 40 days of prayer and fasting we read in Luke 4:14: "Then Jesus returned *in the power of the Spirit* to Galilee". It is one thing *to be filled with the Spirit* and another thing *to be in the power of the Spirit*. When the Lord Jesus was filled with the Spirit, He already possessed the power He needed to exercise His ministry. But it was after the period of prayer and fasting, that power could now freely flow through His life. It flowed to such an extent that Luke 4 continues to say:

[14] ... and news of Him went out through all the surrounding region. [15] And He taught in their synagogues, being glorified by all. [16] So He came to Nazareth, where He had been brought up. And as His custom was, He went into the synagogue on the Sabbath day, and stood up to read. [17] And He was handed the book of the prophet Isaiah. And when He had opened the book, He found the place where it was written: [18]"The Spirit of the LORD is upon Me, Because He has anointed Me To preach the gospel to the poor; He has sent Me to heal the brokenhearted, to proclaim liberty to the captives and recovery of sight to the blind, to set at liberty those who are oppressed; [19] to proclaim the acceptable year of the LORD." [20] Then He closed the book, and gave it back to the attendant and sat down. And the eyes of all who were in the synagogue were fixed on Him. [21] And He began to say to them, "Today this Scripture is fulfilled in your hearing."

It was after being filled with the Spirit and being in the power of the Spirit that the Lord Jesus was indeed the Christ, that is the Anointed One on whom the Holy Spirit was and through whom the Holy Spirit could flow freely for the purposes that are described in the above Scriptures. That is:

- To preach the gospel to the poor.
- To heal the broken-hearted.
- To proclaim liberty to the captives.
- And recovery of sight to the blind.
- To set at liberty those who are oppressed.
- To proclaim the acceptable year of the LORD.

It was as He ministered in the power of the Holy Spirit, and the gospel was preached, and the broken-hearted were healed that *news of Him went out through all the surrounding region.*

The same Holy Spirit that was on the Lord Jesus, He gave to the Church (John 14:14-20, 26; 15:26-27). That is why we may expect that the Church will be a place from where the good news is spread to all its surroundings because of what God is doing in its midst. When we read the Book of Acts we discover that this happened in the early Church. Take for example when Paul and Silas had come to Thessalonica. The Bible says:

Acts 17:6 (NKJV) - ⁶ … "These who have turned the world upside down have come here too."

In other words, the news already had reached Thessalonica of what had happened through the Church in other parts of the then known world. Paul says of the church in Rome:

Romans 1:8 (NKJV) - First, I thank my God through Jesus Christ for you all, that your faith is spoken of throughout the whole world.

Part of the reason that God was moving in such a measure was that news spread from the Church, because prayer and fasting was part of the life of the early believers so that God was able to move freely with His Spirit.

PRAYER IN THE EARLY CHURCH

Just as the Lord Jesus experienced an open heaven and the Holy Spirit descending when He was in prayer, we also see that when the early Church was in prayer the heavens opened and the Holy Spirit descended. It was through the Holy Spirit that the disciples were empowered for the ministry that Jesus had commissioned them to fulfil (Acts 1:8).

Acts 1:12-14 (NKJV) - 12 Then they returned to Jerusalem from the mount called Olivet, which is near Jerusalem, a Sabbath day's journey. 13 And when they had entered, they went up into the upper room where they were staying: Peter, James, John, and Andrew; Philip and Thomas; Bartholomew and Matthew; James the son of Alphaeus and Simon the Zealot; and Judas the son of James. 14 These all continued with one accord in prayer and supplication, with the women and Mary the mother of Jesus, and with His brothers.

In the next verse we can see what the result was of them being in one accord in prayer.

Acts 2:2 (NKJV) - And suddenly there came a sound from heaven, as of a rushing mighty wind, and it filled the whole house where they were sitting.

We have already seen that when the Lord Jesus was in prayer the heavens opened and the Spirit came down. Now we see the Church in prayer and the same thing happened. The heavens opened and the Spirit came down. This is how the Church started; the Church was birthed in prayer. But the Church not only started in prayer; it also continued in prayer.

Acts 2:42 (NKJV) - And they continued steadfastly in the apostles' doctrine and fellowship, in the breaking of bread, and in prayers.

We read of another example of the Church continuing in prayer in the next Scripture:

Acts 4:31 (NKJV) - And when they had prayed, the place where they were assembled together was shaken; and they were all filled with the Holy Spirit, and they spoke the word of God with boldness.

When we sum all these Scriptures up we can state that the Church was born in prayer and that prayer continued to be a vital part of church life. As a result of prayer the early Church saw the Holy Spirit work strongly in their midst and through them to the world.

FASTING IN THE EARLY CHURCH

Acts 13:1-3 (NKJV) - 1 Now in the church that was at Antioch there were certain prophets and teachers: Barnabas, Simeon who was called Niger, Lucius of Cyrene, Manaen who had been brought up with Herod the tetrarch, and Saul. 2 As they ministered to the Lord and fasted, the Holy Spirit said, "Now separate to Me Barnabas and Saul for the work to which I have called them." 3 Then, having fasted and prayed, and laid hands on them, they sent them away.

Acts 14:23 (NKJV) - So when they had appointed elders in every church, and prayed with fasting, they commended them to the Lord in whom they had believed.

In his book, *Fasting*, Brother Derek Prince says that to spread the gospel first of all the apostles were being sent out to preach the gospel. Secondly, the new converts were being placed under the leadership of elders. Both the sending out of the apostles and the appointing of elders were done after they had prayed and fasted. We can conclude that the spreading of the gospel and the growth of the Church were partly the result of fasting. Fasting is one of the ingredients to be a growing and gospel spreading church.

FASTING PREPARES THE WAY FOR THE HOLY SPIRIT

We have already seen that prayer is a major key to experiencing the Holy Spirit in our lives and churches, but adding fasting to it magnifies the effect of our prayers. Let us read the following Scriptures:

Joel 2:15-16 (NIV) - [15] Blow the trumpet in Zion, declare a holy fast, call a sacred assembly. [16] Gather the people, consecrate the assembly; bring together the elders, gather the children, those nursing at the breast. Let the bridegroom leave his room and the bride her chamber.

This scripture is a call to all the people of God to seek God wholeheartedly with fasting. It goes on by saying:

Joel 2:17 (NIV) - Let the priests, who minister before the LORD, weep between the temple porch and the altar. Let them say, "Spare your people, O LORD. Do not make your inheritance an object of scorn, a byword among the nations. Why should they say among the peoples, 'Where is their God?' "

This talks about leaders who are being called to be an example to the people in seeking God. There is a great need for men and women of God who are examples in seeking God in prayer and fasting.

In *Fasting*, Brother Derek Prince also says that in the book of Joel a situation is described where God's people were totally robbed of His glory and power. Israel was not a reflection of God's glory at all any longer. The nations surrounding them asked, 'Where is their God?' It was in this sad situation that God wanted to bring a change, and one of the things God said was that His people needed to pray and fast.

The next verse shows what God promises when His people start to pray and fast:

> Joel 2:28-29 (NIV) - [28]"And afterward, I will pour out my Spirit on all people. Your sons and daughters will prophesy, your old men will dream dreams, your young men will see visions. [29]Even on my servants, both men and women, I will pour out my Spirit in those days."

In other words, God will restore His glory back to His people when they seek Him in prayer and fasting.

> 2 Chronicles 7:14 (NIV) - if My people, who are called by My name, will humble themselves and pray and seek My face and turn from their wicked ways, then will I hear from heaven and will forgive their sin and will heal their land.

CONCLUSION

Maybe it is because prayer and fasting are such important and powerful ingredients of Christian living, and of church life, that they have become Satan's main targets to fight. Maybe that is why Christians and churches struggle to practice it on a regular basis. But now, realising the importance of prayer and fasting, let's rise up and become men and women of prayer and fasting. Let us raise up churches that pray and fast in order for God's Spirit to move freely in us and through us, and that the name of the Lord Jesus Christ will be glorified.

WHY CHURCH UNITY?

Phi 4:2 - I plead with Euodia and I plead with Syntyche to agree with each other in the Lord.

Phi 4:3 - Yes, and I ask you, loyal yokefellow, help these women who have contended at my side in the cause of the gospel, along with Clement and the rest of my fellow workers, whose names are in the book of life.

Disagreements, different opinions and viewpoints on many subjects are a daily occurrence; even in the early Church we see the phenomenon of disagreements between ministers of the gospel and sometimes even arguments. The Apostle Paul introduces two sisters, Euodia and Syntyche. To stop them arguing with each other he gives a very interesting piece of advice; he asks them to be 'of one mind.' He does not ask them to act in the same way, as an army would, marching together in unison dressed in the same manner, with the same step and pace. Instead he asks them to move in harmony.

A choir is the perfect example of harmony, each singer has his own voice, his own tone and his own place in the melody - they do not sing in unison. As they begin singing all together, what is important is the end result. So for the correct result, which is the success of the group, all have to try. The way for this to be achieved is through all being of one mind and having one goal, each person supporting the others and no one in competition. In a choir there are also soloists, but at the time when they are all functioning as a group each singer has to bring his voice, his talent, his energy and his opinion under subjection to get a good result.

The Church has a target and a goal, which is to preach the gospel of salvation to the entire world and to destroy the works of darkness. We sometimes forget something very important which unfortunately the devil does not forget. 'Every kingdom divided against itself will be ruined, and every city or household divided against itself will not stand' (Matt. 12:25). Petty differences can prevent the Church achieving victory.

UNITY AMIDST DIVERSITY (EPH. 4:1-8)

Absolute uniformity, the prohibition of different opinions and the fear of excommunication is not unity, it is dictatorship and religion, and it is a heavy burden. The Apostle Paul advises the Ephesians about what the attitude of each member should be, what the attitude of all the body should be and what the attitude of the leadership should be in order to maintain unity in the Church. This should be a unity that succeeds in uniting people of different personalities, nationalities and ways of life in the Church.

THE ATTITUDE OF EACH MEMBER OF THE GROUP (EPH. 4:1-3)

In Ephesians 4:1, Paul urges the people, 'To live a life worthy of the calling you have received.' This is a general statement and the Apostle Paul goes on to analyze what he means:

1. **With complete humility**

   Humility is not a choice, but an attitude of life. When you are being humble, you do not choose where, when or how (Gal. 2:20). You are humble and you function with humility.

2. **With complete gentleness**

   Prejudice, divisions and disagreements within the Body of Christ always involve anger, rage and selfishness. Gentleness (or meekness) leads by its very nature to reconciliation. Each believer should remember that he has taken on a specific ministry, the ministry of reconciliation (2 Cor. 5:18).

3. **With longsuffering**

   As the word suggests, this is a soul which can stand many insults and many hard blows and when he thinks he has reached the end of his patience, he finds a little more. Unfortunately many Christians are easily angered and readily take offence. They can be touchy and irritable and some become enraged without reason.

If we say we love our brothers then we must not forget that wonderful scripture Col. 3:14 (NIV) – "And over all these virtues put on love, which binds them all together in perfect unity." Basically, the Apostle Paul is showing us how to measure our love. How much love does the Church have, what level has it reached? Unless our attitude and our unity are perfect we cannot put on the love of Christ.

4.   **Bearing with one another in love**
This is the continuation of longsuffering. Here the Apostle Paul simply adds a negative element; the word 'bear' is negative.

It signifies: Burden, load; it means putting up with something that I don't like and may even disagree with.

It signifies: Discontentment because I am doing something which I really do not enjoy at all, but I have to bear it.

It signifies: That what is happening is like a disease that I have to suffer with patience, giving glory to God.

This is the attitude of each one of us towards his brother and while I am bearing, my attitude is one of love. During the period of 'bearing' I do not complain, I do not judge, I do not reject, I do not make lists of what is owed to me, but I love, I am merciful and I bless.

5.   **Making every effort to keep the unity (Zeal)**
We have identified indifference, cowardice and any 'shady' behaviour as harmful to church unity. Shady people want to know what's going on, to gather information without taking sides and do not support the leadership of the church. Zeal requires passion. The people of God should be passionate in their efforts to keep the unity of the Spirit because division and dispute divide the Holy Spirit, His anointing and His presence in the body. If that happens, no side benefits.

THE ATTITUDE OF THE BODY (EPH. 4:4-6)

All the points that the Apostle Paul lays down as to how and where the unity of the Body should be maintained are:

1. One body
2. One hope
3. One Lord
4. One faith
5. One baptism
6. One God and Father

The following elements are not good for Church unity:

1. My ministry.
2. My anointing.
3. Teachings which are of less importance but have become our favourite subjects, let us remember what went on in the days of Timothy (1 Tim. 1:4).
4. Favouritism: following individuals with special gifts and believing that when we are close to them we will be noticed or that we will receive special anointing or spiritual experiences.
5. New revelations and truths that supposedly have never been heard of before. This is actually dangerous for our souls.
6. Religious or church systems that oppress the people and whose only aim is to maintain influence and increase finances.
7. The religious spirit that leads souls into bondage.

All the above lead to the destruction and division of the body and often these can be found behind schisms, impropriety and offence towards the body of Christ.

THE ATTITUDE OF THE LEADERSHIP OF THE CHURCH

The Apostle Paul is trying to build up a group of different people, speaking a different language and having a different culture and history, but also a body unified, in harmony, productive and blessed. He knew very well that the unity of the Church gives great pleasure to the heart of the

Father and when our heavenly Father is pleased, then His blessing and His presence among us is sure.

He did certain things which we should copy:

1. He built up people and not his own kingdom by using people. Unfortunately many Pastors have fallen into the trap of thinking about their churches as a businessman would think about his business. This mentality is wrong - it says I use people and when I have taken (or they have given me) what they have I discard them like rubbish. We are to build up people, families and ministers, not knock them down.

2. He was not afraid to confront people who were causing trouble in the Church. Do not seek short-term peace because that will sentence you to a long-term war. When dealing with every issue in the church, whether moral or disciplinary, we must use the principles of the gospel.

3. He chose co-workers who had the same heart, such as Timothy (Phil.2:20-21). He calls him 'isopsychon' which means being the same as or having the same soul as him. This does not mean having the same theology or agreement in style of government. He trusted Timothy not because of his gifting or his abilities but because he had developed a close relationship with him. He knew that Timothy would act, love, discipline and bless the Church just as the Apostle Paul himself would. What the Apostle Paul did with Timothy condemns, or at least raises questions about, the practice of many leaders today. All these leaders, instead of promoting people to positions of authority whom they know and have built healthy relationships with, employ leaders as if they were running a business. Eventually we all pay for such mistakes. Do not choose leaders according only to gifting, abilities and talents.

4. The Apostle Paul looked for the strengths of his co-workers: each completed the other. There was a spirit of teamwork and cooperation and they functioned in harmony.

5. The next important practice of the Apostle Paul when choosing co-workers was to teach them and to make them participants in his vision. They knew in which direction they were heading and what the Apostle Paul demanded from them. In this way he was sure of success because they were walking together, not just in the same direction but they were also aligned with him.

6.   Everyone knew their true reward; they knew exactly what they were going to get from their ministry. The Apostle Paul did not give his co-workers vague promises or impressions about the future; his life was their example.

CONCLUSION

What the Devil did not manage through persecution, fear and violence against the Christians and the Church, he managed through jealousy, division and pride. The warning of the Apostle Paul is possibly even more urgent and true today than it has ever been before.

Acts 20:28-31 - "Even from among your own number men will arise and distort the truth in order to draw away disciples after them"

Through the unity of the Church we receive this picture:

1 Peter 2:5 - "You also, like living stones, are being built into a spiritual house to be a holy priesthood…."

The unified church is a house, where its 'stones' are built; they have found their position. Each one knows where and how to help and knows their own value and the burden they must lift.

If though, as occurs in many churches, those stones are just laid around scattered in the field then the house is not built and passers-by can take whatever they like from it and however many stones they want. This is very painful for the people of God, grieves the Holy Spirit and instead of leading to spiritual blessing it leads to misery.

The unity of the members of each local church is the joy of the Father, their God who commands His blessing. In order for this to be achieved it requires a lot of hard work, wisdom, effort and sacrifice. It is not an automatic procedure, because standing against the unity of the Church are the armies of Satan.

Chapter 17 – Chip Kawalsingh

Preaching With A Purpose

One of the greatest needs today is effective Bible preaching that connects with the heart of men and brings them closer to God. The Apostle Paul comments on his own preaching in:

1 Corinthians 2:1-5 (NIV) - [1] When I came to you, brothers, I did not come with eloquence or superior wisdom as I proclaimed to you the testimony about God. [2] For I resolved to know nothing while I was with you except Jesus Christ and him crucified. [3] I came to you in weakness and fear, and with much trembling. [4] My message and my preaching were not with wise and persuasive words, but with a demonstration of the Spirit's power, [5] so that your faith might not rest on men's wisdom, but on God's power.

There are many preachers today who rest on human wisdom and eloquence and not enough on the power of God through the person of the Holy Spirit. Now, resting on God's power is not an excuse for poor study habits, 'last minute Saturday night' messages or sloppiness on the platform (Ezra 7:10; Proverbs 13:4; 20:4; 26:24; 2 Timothy 2:15).

In the natural, words are very important. They can come to signify life or death. If someone has been knocked unconscious, one of the first things looked for after their eyes open is a word. Words come to signify life. It is the same in preaching; our words can bring life and hope in everyday tough situations.

Preachers have the greatest job on the earth; we are called to deliver the greatest message, which is God's Word. So we must rightly divide the Word, know the Word and study to show ourselves approved. There are no short cuts to this; it will take fasting, much prayer and time alone with God. In Acts 6:1-6 we see the severity of the need of the Word in that the disciples chose faithful men to carry on with the other needful things while they focused on prayer and the Word.

When we preach, it should be life changing, alive and fun! We should see the fruit of the Word in people's lives as well as our own. We don't preach to be liked, or preach what people want to hear, but we preach God's word. There is a generation today that only wants to hear comforting, positive and uplifting messages. Now these should be ingredients of a great message, but not the whole message all of the time (2 Timothy 4:3-4).

REASONS FOR PREACHING

Romans 10:14 (NKJV) - How then shall they call on Him in whom they have not believed? And how shall they believe in Him of whom they have not heard? And how shall they hear without a preacher?

The Greek word used here for preacher is *kērussō* (pronounced: *kay-roos'-so)* and it means to *herald* (as a public *crier*), especially divine truth (the gospel; proclaim, publish).

When we preach, we should have a goal, aim and a point to the message. It should flow and be easy to understand, backed up with scripture, facts and humour to drive the point home. It should be seasoned with grace and marinated with the Holy Spirit. When all these things come together, the heart of both sinner and saint is touched by God. Here are the reasons we should be preaching:

1. **To Encourage, Exhort and Comfort**

    This not only applies to prophecy, but to the spoken word. When we encourage people, it's not that we are saying it's ok to live the way you are, but rather encouraging one another in faith to move to a higher level in God. In a world where things are constantly changing, where fear and uncertainty are all around us, we must have a message of faith and hope that shows that God still sits on the throne and He is still in control (Romans 4:19; Ephesians 4:12 & 1 Thessalonians 5:11).

2. **To Bring Instruction and Equip the Saints**

    This is not only in spiritual matters, but in daily living. The Word of God is complete and lacking nothing, it contains all we need to live life on the earth today. Because of sin, man's heart has been blinded by the god of this age (2 Corinthians 4:4) and we need the Word and the Holy Spirit to help remove the veil from people's eyes, helping them to make better life choices and make adjustments to be pleasing to God (Ephesians 4:14-16).

3. **To Bring Correction**

We live in a time where sound doctrine is no longer common, the result of which is many different misunderstandings of Scriptures. In the Great Commission in Matthew 28:19 - 20, we have been given the command by Jesus to teach them to obey everything that He has commanded us, this will include bringing correction to wrong living and faulty doctrine (1 Timothy 6:3; 2 Timothy 3:16; 4:3; Titus 1:9; Hebrews 6:1-2; 13:9; 2 Peter 2:1).

4. **To Build The Church**

Preaching is more than winning souls; it is for building the Church. We are called to be wise master builders (1 Corinthians 3:10), building on the right foundations. As we lay the right foundations, the Church (people) will be built together as one people, a spiritual house of which we are all part, as living stones (1 Peter 2:4-10).

The Personal Life of the Preacher

As a cake or dish will have many ingredients in it to make it tasty, so it is with the preparation and delivery of a sermon. Remember, God created you and called you into ministry! As He has called you, so He will also equip you. When preaching, you will learn and pick up many things to help you be a great communicator, but it's important to be you and not to try and copy someone else.

Before you prepare your sermon, have a goal and know exactly what it is you are trying to communicate. Knowing the type of audience you will be speaking to will help, although this is not totally necessary.

Much prayer, fasting and reading of the Word should take place every day of your life. It is important to understand you don't just pray, fast and read the Word to get a sermon, but also to equip you and fill your own personal well. You cannot give out if your well is dry; every day you need fresh oil and Word in your life.

Learn to study the Bible, rightly dividing the Word. There are many resources available at MFE that will help you to become a better student of the Word, but nothing will prepare you more than your own personal walk with God and his Word.

Acts 4:31 (NLT) - After this prayer, the meeting place shook, and they were all filled with the Holy Spirit. Then *they preached the word of God with boldness*.

Geoffrey Thomas, in *The Preacher and Preaching* said, "One reason the gates of hell are not falling before the church is our lack of boldness in preaching…We are not wielding the sword of the Spirit, but the baton of a conductor."

Our personal walk with the Holy Spirit as believers, Pastors and preachers is paramount to boldness, freshness and the anointing on our preaching and leadership. The Holy Spirit was sent by Jesus as our comforter, help, advocate, and the truth giver (John 14:15-31).

The Holy Spirit prompts us in our preaching, focuses us on the need and helps us connect with the heart of man. The pulpit should never be used to adjust someone, deal with people's problems or address a specific problem in church. We preach God's Word from the pulpit and shepherd the flock one on one. Without the Holy Spirit's guidance, our preaching will fall to the ground and produce nothing.

THE APPEAL AFTER THE PREACHED WORD

My spiritual father Colin Cooper once said to me in the early days of my preaching, "Son you are a great preacher but you're not reeling in the fish!" In other words I had done all the work, put the preparation in, and with help of the Holy Spirit, touched the heart of man, but I was not asking the right questions at the end and giving an opportunity for people to respond to God's Word.

I have since learnt that lesson and have now passed this on to our leaders that, no matter what we do, always give an appeal for souls and for people to change their ways.

You can spend lots of time on the preparation and delivery of a sermon but not enough on the ending. The end is as important as the beginning. You need to give the sinner a chance to give their heart to Jesus and for the troubled saint to repent and turn back to God.

Here are some practical pointers:

1. **Know When To Stop!**

   Delay at the end can cause people to lose concentration on what you were actually saying. It can also lead to frustration! Think about it like a flight, if the pilot was to announce, "ladies and gentlemen, we will be landing in 10 minutes", but then he was to continue on for another 25 minutes, the passengers would get restless, fed up and anxious!

   Your conclusion should be to the point, getting the people ready for their hearts to be recaptured with the main message. At this time you can invite your keyboard player or one main musician up to play quietly in the background. Too many people moving around can be distracting, so keep it to one for this time. Have a song in mind or ask your worship director to prepare something beforehand.

2. **Ask The Right Questions**

   Be clear as to what you are asking of the people - it's important that you're not vague. If you are going to ask the church to repeat a prayer after you, know exactly what you're going to say.

   Have a prayer team ready to help pray for the people. The prayer team should be leaders who have been trained in how to pray and minister to people. You don't want the prayer team giving the individual a mini-sermon, just to pray with them. Prophecy should be avoided and only given by those who are qualified to do so. It is good practice to have the men pray with men and for ladies to pray with the ladies.

3. **Have a Follow up Team in Place**

   It's important once the sinner has responded, that you have a follow-up team ready to help disciple that individual. This team should be trained on how to counsel a new believer. They should have Bibles and new materials ready to give to each new believer. It's not enough to just have the raised hand and to leave that new believer to fend for themselves. You need to have someone to connect with them, walk with them and help them on this new incredible journey.

   Also, it would be great to have a time where all the new converts and those new to your church can come together for a time of fun, food and fellowship. You can then follow up with teaching on water baptism, membership classes, and eventually disciple them towards becoming a fellow builder in the church.

CONCLUSION

Preaching can be effective, fun and fulfilling. There are no short cuts, but by God's grace you can take that gift that the Lord has given you and develop it to such a level that it brings sinners to Jesus and helps saints to be more like Christ. Anything you do in life will call for sacrifice, hard work and discipline. Today, determine in your heart that you will become a preacher of purpose.

CHAPTER 18 – GORDON TOSE

BUILDING LOYALTY WITHIN YOUR LEADERSHIP

There are many ingredients that are needed to make an effective leadership team. One of the most important of these is loyalty. Many a team, made up of gifted men and women, has failed to fulfil its potential, and has even been rendered ineffective because of a lack of this essential ingredient. The problem in teaching on the subject of loyalty is that everyone assumes that they are loyal. We don't need loyalty building into us because it's already there, it's already a part of what we are, and yet the Bible says:

Proverbs 20:6 (Good News) - "Everyone talks about how loyal and faithful he is, but just try and find someone who really is."

Of course, in reality, loyalty is birthed out of relationship and the most important relationships in any church are those that exist between the Senior Pastor and their support leadership. It would be helpful to clarify that the role of the support leadership, as obvious as this may seem, is to support the Senior Pastor. It has no other role.

1Chronicles 12:16-18 (NIV) - "Other Benjamites and some men from Judah also came to David in his stronghold. David went out to meet them and said to them, "If you have come to me in peace, to help me, I am ready to have you unite with me. But if you have come to betray me to my enemies when my hands are free from violence, may the God of our fathers see it and judge you". Then the Spirit came upon Amasai, chief of the Thirty, and he said, "We are yours, O David! We are with you, O son of Jesse! Success, success to you, and success to those who help you, for your God will help you." So David received them and made them leaders of his raiding bands."

So here we have David in exile in Ziklag, and he is joined by an army of warriors. You will note that he specifically asks them if they have come to help him and to support him.

"If you have come to me in peace, to help *me*"

It wasn't a case, putting this in a church setting, of asking them if they had come to join him, for example, in doing the work of God. David was very clear as to where their allegiance should be, which was to him personally and not to their own agenda. They knew exactly what David was asking which is why they replied as they did.

"We are yours, O David! We are with you, O son of Jesse!"

The whole focus of their response was on David and not on God. Again, in a church setting, it wasn't "I'm committed to God, and as long as you and I appear to want the same things we will walk together." They were committing themselves to David. Committing ourselves to someone is very easy to express but it's a lot more difficult to live out.

An obvious question to ask is, was theirs a reasonable response? Maybe they didn't mean it. Maybe it was said out of their desperation to have David as their leader. We see in response to David's demand that the Holy Spirit revealed to Amasai that David was indeed God's man. What Amasai was saying was that in committing themselves to David, in following David, they were in fact committing themselves to, and following, God.

"Success, success to you, and success to those who help you, for your God will help you."

David made them leaders because of their commitment. Any leader, in whatever capacity, undoubtedly needs to be gifted as such. To make someone a leader based solely on their gift is dangerous, for without commitment, ahead lays disappointment and sometimes conflict.

When the support leadership team functions as it should it has real benefits, not just for the Pastor but for the church as a whole. We see this in the relationship between Moses and Aaron. When God appointed Aaron to a position of authority among the Israelites, he was appointed to help Moses in the task that God had given Moses to do. We see a wonderful example of this in Exodus 17:8-15 where Moses is on a hill overlooking a battle between the Israelites and the Amalekites, and he is interceding with God on behalf of his people. Whilst Moses held his arms high, the Israelites had the upper hand, but as soon as his arms began to tire the tide turned in favour of the Amalekites. Aaron and Hur, therefore, stood either side of Moses and prevented his arms from falling and in doing so ensured Israel's victory. In that whole battle it is important to understand who God was listening to. He wasn't listening to Aaron and Hur, neither was He listening to Joshua even though it's Joshua who was doing the actual fighting. No, God was listening to Moses, and Moses alone. These other men were important, but their importance lay in their willingness to support their leader.

It is certainly true that Aaron was appointed because Moses, by himself, wasn't up to the job that God had for him. In fact the prospect of leading the Israelites out of Egypt led Moses to plead with God:

Exodus 4:13 (NIV) - "But Moses said, "O Lord, please send someone else to do it.""

God's response to this plea in verse 16, talking about Aaron is:

"He will speak to the people for you, and it will be as if he were your mouth and as if you were God to him."

This makes it abundantly clear that Aaron's only role was that of supporting Moses. Having said that, there has to be an acknowledgement by senior ministry that they do need support. Moses needed Aaron just as David needed his mighty men. The mighty men would probably never have been mighty without David's leadership, but equally, David would never have accomplished anything without them. That is the beauty and the strength of "Team".

Unfortunately there can also be a negative aspect to "Team" which is why some Senior Pastors don't really want one. They may have a group of people they call a team, but it doesn't function as a team. An effective team is made up of different types of people, which can be both a strength and a weakness. The book of Ephesians chapter 4 seems to suggest that the ideal team should be made up of individuals with apostolic, evangelistic, prophetic, pastoral and teaching giftings. However, it is likely that people with those kinds of gifts are going to have very different temperaments. These differences can and will bring diversity, but they can also lead to differences of opinion. My Pastor and I are completely different. We are different in background, experience and personality. The way that works out is that, from time to time, things are done in a way that I find uncomfortable - and very few of us enjoy moving out of our comfort zones. We all know the story of Gideon's three hundred men who fought the Midianites. To be honest, if I had been in charge, we would probably have done it a different way. So when we are faced with this kind of situation, when we're part of the support team, we have a choice to make. Do we embrace the Biblical principle of submitting to our leader's authority, or do we fight to impose our opinion? The problem with "our opinion" is that we generally assume that we are right, which we may or may not be. The reality is that *opinion without a revelation of authority leads to division.*

Even where there is an understanding of team and a functioning team, it does not mean that all the team members are team players. What does being a team player entail? It certainly entails not competing with the other team members. It also entails maintaining unity in the church by making the effort to get along with the rest of the team. Being a team player means understanding that what the church needs is more important than what we want. Team players also make the effort to ensure good communication with each other and they have no problem submitting to authority. Above all else a team player is interested in the welfare of the church, which requires a degree of humility. There is nothing quite as destructive as pride, which has most certainly destroyed many relationships.

Proverbs 16:18 (NIV) - "Pride goes before destruction, a haughty spirit before a fall."

There has to be an understanding by the support leadership that often the anointing they have, and certainly the opportunity to exercise that anointing, is because of the Senior Pastor.

1 Chronicles 12:18 - "Success, success to you, and success to those who help you, for your God will help you."

If we really understood this then we would be less threatened by other members of the team and we would be less likely to be ambitious. An example of someone who didn't understand this was Miriam who we see, together with Aaron, complaining about Moses.

Numbers 12:1-2 (NIV) - "Miriam and Aaron began to talk against Moses because of his Cushite wife, for he had married a Cushite. " Has the LORD spoken only through Moses?" they asked. "Hasn't he also spoken through us?" And the LORD heard this."

It becomes obvious when we read this account that it is Miriam who has the problem, and whilst she seems to be attacking Moses' wife she is in fact defending her position as prophetess.

"Hasn't he (God) also spoken through us (me)?"

Miriam valued her gifting and she enjoyed being used by God, and so she should. She was also held in high esteem by the Israelites and it seems that her security had shifted from God to her gifting which is a danger to all of us. In the previous chapter we are told that God had taken the anointing that was on Moses and put it on seventy elders who all began to prophesy. Suddenly Miriam wasn't so special anymore and instead of being 'the' prophet, she was just 'a' prophet, and this is chewing away inside her. So she uses the wife of Moses as a way of voicing her complaint, but God intervenes and Miriam suffers the consequences. Four chapters later in Numbers 16, we are told of Korah's rebellion. Korah already had important duties in the Tabernacle but it wasn't enough. Like Miriam he also suffered the consequences and that's because God hates rebellion.

Even in the church, ambition is commonplace. The Bible warns against it.

James 3:15 & 16 (NIV) - "Such wisdom does not come down from heaven but is earthly, unspiritual, of the devil. For where you have envy and selfish ambition, there you find disorder and every evil practice."

The Apostle Paul writes to the elders in the church at Ephesus and warns them.

Acts 20:30 (NIV) - "Even from your own number men will arise and distort the truth in order to draw away disciples after them."

Paul is more than likely referring to those from within their own leadership team. Miriam was part of the team, as was Korah.

Let me say this: over the years, for a lot of the time I was the "second man" in my church for no other reason than there was nobody else. There came a time, however, when two other elders were brought onto the team, neither of whom were novices and both of whom were very gifted. Like Miriam, I wasn't so special anymore. Not being as special is actually not very easy to come to terms with. Thankfully I had an understanding that the reason for much of the blessing in my life was because of my commitment to my Pastor. As far as I was concerned this relationship was more important than any glory I may get from people, which at best is very temporary, and more important than any feeling of self worth I might get from some kind of platform ministry.

Of course, when we talk of our commitment to someone, this should not be on the basis of their perfection. There has to be an understanding from both senior ministry and support ministry that none of us is perfect. In the story of Aaron and the golden calf we find Moses away on a ministry trip with Aaron being left behind in charge of the church. Moses is away much longer than expected and the "sheep" get tired of waiting and it says:

Exodus 32:1 (NIV) - "they gathered around Aaron and said, "Come, make us gods who will go before us.""

So Aaron makes them an idol in the form of a golden calf. If he had been forced into doing this you would think he would protest his innocence by saying he had no choice in the matter. Yet when Moses asks him why he did it, Aaron's response in verses 22-24 is very revealing:

"Do not be angry, my lord," Aaron answered. "You know how prone these people are to evil. They said to me, 'Make us gods who will go before us…' So I told them, 'Whoever has any gold jewellery, take it off.' Then they gave me the gold, and I threw it into the fire, and out came this calf."

So not only did Aaron make a mistake but he then refused to accept responsibility for it, which of course is the end of his ministry! Well, no it wasn't. His ministry continued.

I think most of us in support ministry would expect the backing of our Pastor when we inevitably get things wrong. I think that what we expect and what we sometimes give in return are not always the same. There appears to be an unwritten assumption that the higher you are in leadership, the more perfect you are. This is far from the truth. Leadership is actually a gift from God and gifts are given to us by God as gifts. The gift of being able to function as a Senior Pastor is not earned on the basis of some degree of perfection. If it was, it wouldn't be a gift; it would be ours by right. When the Senior Pastor displays his imperfection, this can be very difficult for the support team to handle.

A great example of senior leader imperfection is King David. Yet despite his weaknesses, some of which were lifestyle issues, God nevertheless was able to look back over David's life and declare in:

1 Kings 14:8 (NIV) - "my servant David, who kept my commands and followed me with all his heart, doing only what was right in my eyes."

Noah is another good example. He was considered righteous by God and yet he got drunk. One of his sons, Ham, finding his father naked on the floor, went and told his two brothers who, in response, *covered their father's nakedness*. The two of them were blessed by God while Ham was cursed, and the whole focus of that incident was not on the incident itself, but on the reaction to it. It is fair to say therefore, in general terms, that a display of someone's imperfection is not grounds for the breaking of relationships or the withdrawing of support.

What we have to realise is that disloyalty is never acceptable to God, no matter what the provocation. David understood this which is why he wouldn't kill Saul when on two separate occasions he had the opportunity. Saul, after having been God's instrument in bringing David to prominence, then became the obstacle between David and the fulfilment of God's plan for him. If David had killed Saul then the obstacle would have been removed and no one would have blamed him. Indeed he was encouraged by his men to do just that.

1 Samuel 24:4 (NIV) - "The men said, "This is the day the LORD spoke of when he said to you, 'I will give your enemy into your hands for you to deal with as you wish.'""

David knew that disloyalty, for this is what it would have been, had its consequences. It is a pity he forgot this principle when it came to Uriah.

In fact nowhere in the Bible does anybody benefit from disloyalty. Miriam was made leprous, Korah was destroyed, and Ham was cursed. Even those who may have felt totally justified in their actions, they too suffered; people like Ahithophel, David's counsellor and friend, but also, importantly, Bathsheba's grandfather. Two things may have helped turn Ahithophel against David. Firstly, David's despicable behaviour towards his granddaughter and her husband. Secondly Absalom's persuasive tongue. Whatever the justification for his actions, it was Ahithophel who ended up committing suicide.

Joab is another example. Simplistically speaking, Joab's relationship with David was one which started well, but one which finished badly. Maybe the turning point in their relationship was when Joab received the letter from David ordering the death of Uriah. The Bible doesn't record how Joab reacted to this instruction but it's likely he didn't view David in a positive light. Nevertheless it was Joab who ended up being assassinated. God, it seems, will never ignore disloyalty. He may forgive it, as he did with David, but He will never ignore it.

What we must realise is that a successful leadership team comes from relationship, not organisation. There also needs to be an understanding of the privileges and the responsibilities that exist within these relationships. The support team have a responsibility to support the Senior Minister and when they understand this there are tremendous benefits, not just for the church corporately, but also for the support team individually. Senior Ministers benefit when they are truly supported, but they have the responsibility of being deserving of that support. Their catch phrase should be that of the Apostle Paul:

1 Corinthians 11:1 (NIV) - "Follow my example, as I follow the example of Christ."

David's mighty men did not blindly follow David. They were fully convinced of the fact that David was God's anointed and God's appointed. When three of his men risked their lives to bring him a drink of water from the well at Bethlehem in 2 Samuel 23, it was because they were willing to sacrifice themselves for a leader who was willing to sacrifice himself for them. Mutual sacrifice, the basis for any successful meaningful relationship.

Psalm 133:1 & 3 (adapted) - How good and pleasant it is when there are no church politics. How good and pleasant it is when leaders understand the importance of relationships, when they understand the importance of maintaining those relationships. For where true unity exists, there the Lord commands His blessing, even life forevermore.

Chapter 19 – Memos Sakellariou

The Importance of Faith

Hebrews 11:6 - "And without faith it is impossible to please God, because anyone who comes to him must believe that he exists and that he rewards those who earnestly seek him".

There was once a painting competition called "Peace" and the judges had to choose between two paintings: the first showed a place which was perfectly quiet with a sunset, clear skies and a man lying on a beach. It was very calm and still. The second picture was the one which won the competition. This showed a bird on the end of a branch, close to a strong-flowing river and almost touching the water. The little bird was chirping merrily whilst the strong current flowed directly below it, leading to a waterfall. This is a perfect illustration of faith – when you trust in God and have faith you can live in the loudest and most dangerous place on Earth and still be completely peaceful and content.

Christians today assess their faith and the Church using different criteria than those used by the Apostle Paul. If someone asks us, "How is your church doing?" what do you think he is really asking, and what is our reply? Nearly everyone is interested in learning the following: How many members there are in the local church, what the annual increase in number of members is in the church and how the building programme is going. They also want to know whether the church members live holy lives, based on them not drinking alcohol, not smoking and not committing adultery or other sins.

When the Apostle Paul sent Timothy to the church in Thessalonica he wanted to learn something much more important: the level of faith of the church (1 Thess. 3:2-10).

We should remember that there were two things which we are told surprised Jesus, things he was amazed by more than anything else in His earthly ministry: (Luke 7:9, Matt.15:28). Firstly the great faith He found in the hearts of certain people. He was not impressed by their righteousness or their holiness. Secondly he was shocked by lack of faith (Mark 6:5-6, Matt. 9:29). Nothing amazed Jesus as much as lack of faith; this amazed Him more than sin, disobedience or lack of respect.

WHAT IS FAITH? (HEBREWS 11:1-3)

It is total dependency on God which produces a different kind of vision. This is because with faith we see further, beyond our circumstances; we see Jesus beside us in all our needs. Take note of the fact that faith is more than words.

We are sometimes given the impression that faith is just saying the right words, speaking positively or making positive confessions; or it may be to repeat scriptures on healing, prosperity or whatever blessing is required. Unfortunately this is like using a "magic word" or "magic vision". This teaching has led people to stop praying because they must not admit that they have needs or that they are ill. The faith that God calls us to have is not based on a denial of reality (Phil.4:19-20).

Abraham, when faced by the reality of his situation, chose to stand on the promises of God and he believed in the Lord. The most blessed Christian is not the one who has succeeded the most but the one who has received the most. This is why the Apostle Paul felt safer when he was feeling weak because then he was sure of God's strength (2 Cor.12:9-10).

FAITH: THE KEY TO OUR RELATIONSHIP WITH THE LORD (1 PETER 1:5)

It is faith which releases the power of God. Faith is the key in our relationship with God, and it is this key that Satan tries, with his evil tricks, to steal. This is why we see believers losing their first love, the love that made us feel ready to do absolutely anything for Christ. This is why we see people with the call of God on their life, who started off on fire for God, now wandering around cold. It can even happen to Pastors who begin with a vision, anointing and passion for the work of God and now find themselves disappointed, this is spiritual and physical burnout.

Faith is a journey, a daily walk in the promises that God has given us. We should not look only at the circumstances around us and we should not allow our emotions to direct us. We look for an example to Abraham, the father of faith. Abraham lived standing on the promises of God and not simply following the commandments. The promises of God bring hope to our hearts: faith steps happily into the unknown knowing who is walking alongside. We feel safe when we know exactly what is going to happen beforehand, where we are heading, and we want to be in control. Faith, on the other hand, is satisfied knowing only that God never fails in the promises He has given. Faith does not worry; neither does it lead us to impatience. We should simply leave the promises in God's hands, through prayer.

We should note that the Lord does not need our help, because He can fulfil His promises and complete His plans. It may be that we should pay careful attention as to whom we share our problems with, especially when those problems are financial. Often we fall into the trap of our own "cleverness" and we manipulate people and situations.

An Atmosphere of Faith

The church's battle is always the same, and the leadership's task is to lead the people of God into a life of faith, whilst working hard at the same time to maintain that high level of faith. This is because it is as we maintain a high level of faith that the promises of God begin to be fulfilled, which in turn makes us stronger. Satan knows that 'the just shall live by faith', so he fights to steal our faith from us. We should remember that faith is not a simple mental acceptance of the truths of the Bible: true faith is produced when our hearts are drawn closer to God and we accept His promises deep in our hearts, then His word produces faith in us though His divine power.

We maintain an atmosphere of faith by:

1. **Devoting time to prayer**
    This is the reason that the Lord said that His house will be called a house of prayer. Prayer opens the channels of blessing. God draws near when His people pray; He enjoys communicating with His people. So we teach the church to pray, then, when they have finished praying, the next step is to pray again!

2. **Overcoming disappointment by using the promises of God as a weapon**

Remember the story of the twelve spies in Canaan. They returned with a 'bad report' to Moses and the people (Numbers 13 v. 32). Why was the report 'bad'? It was because it was a report full of fear, unbelief and disappointment which then filled the hearts of the people. Let us be careful, then, to avoid speaking words which are foolish or just from our own thoughts. In contrast we should speak whatever the Lord has given to us as promises.

In our meetings we should be careful not to allow spirits of disappointment to lead. Each of us already has enough disappointment in himself! The Holy Spirit is our comforter and He encourages us to gain and cultivate persistent faith which will be able to stand throughout all difficulties, disappointments and even delays.

3. **Remembering that the leaders provide the example by their own lives**

When we are not hesitant to 'get out of our boat of security' the people are encouraged.

4. **Teaching the people not to react when God takes us out of our comfort zone and habits**

The Lord disciplines us and allows pressures and difficulties in our lives and when this happens we should react correctly. It is through these pressures that we realise what level of faith we are at, and how lacking we really are. When God puts us in certain situations which are over and beyond our strength, He has a reason. Actually He is trying to teach us to trust Him. So we must learn not to fight or to resist the process that God uses, but to wait as grounded, stable and grateful Christians full of faith. It is certain that God wants us to change; He wants us to increase, not to remain the same as we are today.

5. **Teaching the church to follow the promises of God**

This does not mean each person following their own desires. The commandments of God reveal His character and our own weaknesses and sinfulness. These commandments do not have the power to lead us into obedience. So the Christian knows the commandments of God, wants to do what is right but cannot succeed (Romans 7:18). Our problem is where to find the spiritual strength to obey the commandments. This blessed secret is found in 2 Peter 1:4. It is the promises that attract our hearts closer to the Lord and give us the strength to believe. Therefore strong faith requires food; this food is the promises of God. So our food is the Word, it is this Word that we give to the church: the hearing of the Word increases, gives birth to, and feeds faith.

6. **Not allow the church to forget past blessings**

   Teach the people to thank and praise God for yesterday (Heb. 13:15). Teach the people to discuss and remember the promises and also God's answers to prayer.

7. **Teaching the church to look ahead, expecting to obtain all that it has not yet gained**

   There is still ground which has not yet been gained. Do not allow yourself to camp where you are now and feel that you have reached your destination. Remember that faith works in conjunction with two things (Heb. 11:1):

   a. With what we are hoping for
   b. With what we cannot see

   This means that faith is not for the present, it is about things to do with the future, whatever has been promised by God. Faith is also the ability of the human spirit to open up and accept pictures and impressions from God. Unfortunately many Christians today do not believe that God can do something new in their church and consider anything of this nature to be extreme emotionalism. This is called religious tradition; instead let us learn to be daring and to believe.

8. **Teaching the church to "fix our eyes on Jesus" (Hebrews 12:2)**

   Satan wants us to look continually at the problems. We should learn to look to our provider. Unfortunately believers do not always understand the vital connection that exists between prayer and the promises of God, so they stop praying. Unfortunately prayer becomes a 'have to', a duty. When our hearts are full of true, living faith, then there is assurance in our heart as to how we should ask in prayer and receive. Of course we mean prayer which is something more than the reading of a prayer-list. When we learn to wait on the Lord in His presence, when we spend time loving Him, then our faith is developed. Then our heart wants to listen to His voice and is ready to obey and believe.

CONCLUSION

Beloved, how is our church doing? How strong is it? The Apostles once answered the paralysed man (Acts 3:6), "Silver or gold I do not have, but what I have I give you. In the name of Jesus Christ of Nazareth, walk." Today the Church cannot say that; it cannot say, "Silver or gold I do not have" because the Church as a whole *does* have money. At the same time however, it lacks the same power and anointing as was on the Apostles.

A strong church is one which lives its first love, it is one which worships, which looks at the Saviour, which waits as long as necessary to hear His voice and is ready to follow Him wherever He asks. The strong church gazes at the Saviour, Jesus uplifted among the people, and with absolute trust, follows Him.

A HOUSE OF EXCELLENCE

Everything we do for God should be our best. Exodus 23:19 "Bring the best …to the house of the Lord your God." Although the context of this has to do with offerings, the principle is that the best should be in the house. As Pastors we are responsible for bringing a spirit of excellence into everything we do in and outside the church. Church should be fun, exciting, and life changing. It is possible to do this with a spirit of excellence. I have listed some of the great ingredients of successful church services. Much more could be said about each topic; however I have kept these brief so as to whet your appetite for what is needed in a church service.

1. **Prayer**

   This includes meetings such as leader's prayer, pre-service prayer, all-church prayer and prayer and fasting meetings.

   Prayer is done with the purpose of accessing God's favour and blessing by calling out to Him.

   All meetings should start on time. If you are waiting for people to come in every week before starting then you are devaluing the time of the persons who have attended punctually. No matter what culture or country they come from, people have to get to work on time. If they can get to work on time then they should be able to come to church on time, which means you start on time.

   In a prayer meeting setting, a real presence of God is needed as various prayers are offered up to God. Have a plan before your prayer meeting; if you are planning to ask people at random to pray out loud it's a good idea to make sure that the person is happy to hold a microphone and pray out loud in front of people. This can bring total fear to some people. On the other hand some people love to hear their own voice. To have one person who takes over the meeting by praying long winded prayers is distracting and shows a lack of respect for the leader of that meeting. Give clear instruction and guidance before you invite anyone to the microphone. It is often a good idea to have your musicians playing some appropriate music that can help with the atmosphere of the meeting.

2.   Worship

We live in a Christian culture of what I call 'performance-driven worship.' This worship seems to have less to do with God and more to do with the band, style or worship leader. It is not wrong to have excellence in worship; in fact we expect the musicians to be well practised, have good voices and be well presented, however these factors are not as important as the presence of God.

> Exodus 33:15-16 (NLT) - [15] Then Moses said, "If you don't personally go with us, don't make us leave this place. [16] How will anyone know that you look favourably on me—on me and on your people—if you don't go with us? For your presence among us sets your people and me apart from all other people on the earth."

Moses even points out that the distinguishing mark of the believer is the Presence of God. The number one concern of the music group and worship team must be the Presence of God. Nothing else will bring the results we are looking for, and it is through heartfelt worship that we invite Him in.

3.   Word

As we get more and more into technology we have somehow lost a vital part of church life: reading the Word. Do not be so caught up in using PowerPoint graphics that you stop asking people to turn to the scriptures in their Bibles; if you do then the people will not bring their Bibles to church. You can use PowerPoint to only show the address of the verses you wish to refer to, and then the people will bring their Bibles with them. Encourage your people to take notes, writing things down as the Word is given. The Word is the number one ingredient for breaking sin in our lives, without it we are just in a self-help programme that will never bring freedom.

Psalm 119:11 (NLT) - I have hidden your word in my heart that I might not sin against you.

If these basics are kept in church with relevance and dynamism then church life will blossom.

Now in the next part I want to cover what is done from the pulpit. This is for all those who function as leaders in the house of God and covers the area of proper pulpit and platform etiquette. We want to avoid the appearance of evil and make sure that we promote God in a godless generation. As we are 'up front' we need to avoid certain things that can cause the 'cringe factor' or embarrassment to those in the congregation.

Our goal is to build the house of God and promote Jesus in our lives, Church and city.

Please hear the Spirit of things being said; this is in no way a religious legalistic system but rather a heart that wants to promote a house of excellence as our God is a God of excellence.

GUIDELINES FOR THE PLATFORM

1. **Personal Appearance**

    To promote a house and indeed a God of excellence: as a minister of the gospel, or as a person involved in presentation of the church, you should be dressed appropriately, modestly and look presentable.

2. **Attitude in Countenance**

    We are to edify and lift up the name of Jesus. Be positive and create an atmosphere that is Godly. Smile and be welcoming.

3. **Pray Before**

    Whether acting as master of ceremonies, leading worship, preaching or teaching please find the heart of God. Think through what you are doing from the beginning to the end. Please end your sermons or teaching on a positive note. Using a praise song is always good. Go for souls; God can use you to lead others to Him, make appeals for salvation.

DISCRETION FROM 'UP FRONT' OR THE PULPIT

Remember that we are God's mouthpiece. Always ask yourself in any situation: would Jesus say or do that?

1.   Inappropriate Gestures and Movements
   a.   Avoid constant pacing up and down, like a lion in a cage.
   b.   Hold the microphone properly. If you are not sure of the correct way to hold a microphone, ask a public address person for advice.
   c.   Be aware of your gestures.
   d.   Do not ask people onto the stage without warning; some people's greatest fear is of public speaking so pre-plan your meetings and give people plenty of warning of what you intend to do.

2.   Coarse Language
   a.   Avoid jokes about different ethnic groups or crude remarks.
   b.   Avoid sexual innuendos.
   c.   Avoid beating or condemning the people: discipline should happen behind the scenes, not from the pulpit.

WHAT TO PROMOTE IN THE PULPIT

1.   Salvation and the name of Jesus
2.   The Word and Spirit
3.   The Presence of God
4.   Relationships within the Church
5.   The safety of the people
6.   Love and respect for our Pastors and leaders
7.   Love for one another
8.   Meeting together
9.   Faith
10.   Joy

INTRODUCING A GUEST SPEAKER AND LOOKING AFTER GUEST MINISTERS

One of the areas we need to work on is how we treat the guest speakers and ministers invited to our church. Now although this will often mean that you spend some money, it is more than the money. It is having a heart of gratitude that chooses to bless the guest rather than to just make do with what is available.

HOW TO INTRODUCE YOUR GUEST SPEAKER

1. Get their name(s) right (if you are unsure ask them beforehand).
2. Know exactly their church name or organisation.
3. Give honour where honour is due.
   Avoid being over familiar in your introduction about them, although you may be very friendly with them. How you introduce them will determine how your people receive them. Recognise what they do and what they have done.

LOOKING AFTER YOUR GUEST

Make sure they have plenty of help on the way to your church. A good thing to think about, if they are coming from overseas, is to cover their airfare, or at least part of it if you cannot afford the whole amount. It is also a good idea to accommodate them in a hotel if you are able. Many guests will appreciate this, although they would be happy staying in a nice home as an alternative. It is a blessing for Spiritual Fathers and fellow Pastors to go back to a hotel room or nice comfortable home and relax after a meeting.

If they are driving to your church service, have a parking space reserved for them, and offer them a drink or snack upon arrival.

Think about the honorarium ahead of time: the amount is totally up to you; however you should always err on the side of generosity rather than being stingy.

1 Timothy 5:17 (The Message) - Give a bonus to leaders who do a good job, especially the ones who work hard at preaching and teaching. Scripture tells us, "Don't muzzle a working ox" and "A worker deserves his pay."

I really believe that our churches prosper when we are generous to others, especially those who are fellow ministers of the gospel. Every church should show extra care and attention to those guests who are considered to be spiritual fathers. I believe because of the years of service and sacrifice that these men and women have given to the Kingdom, they should be treated with the highest honour and respect. If they are truly spiritual leaders they will not expect to be treated this way; however, it is a sign to God and to them that we honour and love them by what we do for them and give them. Bless your visiting speakers.

Ephesians 6:1-3 (NLT) - [1] Children, obey your parents because you belong to the Lord, for this is the right thing to do. [2] "Honour your father and mother." This is the first commandment with a promise: [3] If you honour your father and mother, "things will go well for you, and you will have a long life on the earth."

NOT DEMANDING ANYTHING

If you have been invited to a church and you are able to go, you should go with humility and with a spirit to serve the people and the Pastors of that church. Do not go with a list of demands or seeking to dictate to the church. Honour what is in your diary first: do not cancel an appointment for a better opportunity or bigger church elsewhere. Accept what is given to you with all kindness and gratitude. Take a small gift to say thank you for whatever they do for you. Do not demand anything but go with a heart to serve and build relationships with that church and its Pastors.

2 Corinthians 11:7-9 (NLT) - [7] Was I wrong when I humbled myself and honoured you by preaching God's Good News to you without expecting anything in return? [8] I "robbed" other churches by accepting their contributions so I could serve you at no cost. [9] And when I was with you and didn't have enough to live on, I did not become a financial burden to anyone. For the brothers who came from Macedonia brought me all that I needed. I have never been a burden to you, and I never will be.

Chapter 21 – Colin Cooper

The Heart Of MFE

Today, all over the world, there are conferences, leaders' training days, discipleship courses, committees, teams, all of them headed up by people with various titles – Apostle, Director, Bishop, Chairman, Prophetic Leader, Senior Pastor and many others. These all belong to a denomination or group, perhaps with some prophetic-named title or maybe an apostolic sounding name. Whatever the title, the organisation tends to reflect what they do in that name. So we have endless groups, denominations and names to choose from.

Now here is another name "Ministers Fellowship Europe". What is it? What does it reflect? What is the heart of Ministers Fellowship Europe? Well the name reflects the ethos of MFE.

Ministers - Fellowship - Europe

The emphasis is on fellowship. Although much has been spoken and written on fellowship by leaders over the years, there is little real, intimate relationship in spite of hearing the Greek noun "*koinonia*" repeatedly. Relationships in general have been shallow – so the heart of MFE is relationship, relationship, relationship, relationship and then after that it's relationship. Many leaders, even when they are part of a group or denomination, feel alone. We have a motto in MFE: *Why Walk Alone When We Can Walk Together?* It is about having others who can walk with you in tough times and give encouragement. MFE is a place where we can be open and accountable. Now I have been in a denomination which encouraged openness and accountability but when you were transparent about your weaknesses they were eventually used against you. MFE is a place where I have found security, where I can be open and transparent, and where my relationships continue without any of my weaknesses being exploited for any reason. Ephesians 4:1-3 tells us to live a life worthy of our calling and to bear with each other in love.

My dearest friend Memos Sakellariou from Athens, Greece, must have watched some of the dumb things that I have done and despaired, but he bears with me. He has patience, loves me and respects me and so, rather than prising us apart, bearing with me has deepened our relationship. Of course that principle has functioned both ways and gives lasting satisfaction and security when you know for certain you have real friends in times of trouble. This gives you courage to face anything, because your friends are with you in any crisis, whether spiritual or practical.

The reality is we were created to walk with friends. Scientists tell us that those individuals who live the longest are the ones with deep friendships. Science simply confirms what the Creator said. In fact, Jesus said the same things to the disciples - John 15:13 "I have called you My friends". Because of past hurts, some leaders retreat into a self-defensive shell and become isolated. This is a very dangerous place to be; many have fallen morally, financially or developed nervous disorders because there was nobody to speak into their lives, or for them to call on during temptation or pressure. In MFE, relationships have been built across the continent as leaders get to know each other in the conferences. They visit each other, minister in each other's churches and encourage each other.

CONFERENCES

Conferences are held each year on a rotation system so that a few European countries host them. Excellent teachers and preachers from Europe, Africa, India, the USA and many other countries come as guests to minister to and build-up conference delegates. Regional conferences are also held - for example Greece holds a Balkan conference each year, the Netherlands and other countries hold them annually for that region. In the UK there are two regional meetings in Spring and Autumn, along with another one for senior leaders. There is also an affiliation with MFI USA, Brazil, Africa, Australia, Philippines and India. If you are a member of MFE then you are free to attend any of the affiliated conferences worldwide. What a great family of churches MFE is!

RESOURCES

Resources are plentiful. Books written by MFE members and books written by famous authors, along with teaching CDs by international speakers and MFE members are sent each quarter to all MFE members. Also 'papers' are regularly sent on any phenomena or happening which has been studied by top Biblical scholars. They are sent to help us understand whether it is error or true revival. Not only are these great resources sent, but often a page of jokes is also included so you can start with a good laugh at the beginning of a sermon! All this and more is sent through something called a 'seed bag' every quarter. MFE's heart is also to be a resource for its members.

RELATIONSHIP

As MFE is relational, no one can join just because they would like to. So how does a leader link in? Well he has to be sponsored by an MFE member who will vouch for his character and integrity. He will also not be a part of another organisation or denomination. So this keeps the integrity of MFE, and means it is built on relationships. MFE's heart is all based on relationships as we have said.

AUTHORITY

MFE does not have authority over any Pastor or church, nor are there any controls imposed. Any input would come at the church leader's request, and any team member invited into that church would still be ultimately under the authority of the local leadership. The churches are autonomous but not independent because of the affiliation. No buildings are owned by MFE and no attempt would ever be made by MFE to try to obtain ownership, as some denominations are in the practice of doing. Being in MFE is to have cover without control; final decisions will always be made by the local leadership.

THE LOCAL CHURCH

MFE places a high priority on building the Local Church. 1 Timothy says the Church of the Living God is the pillar and foundation of the truth - not women's gatherings, men's organisations, student groups, events or travelling to see supernatural happenings. Remember 10% of scripture talks about the worldwide body of believers, but 90% of scripture talks about the local church, so we should emphasise what scripture emphasises.

Local church is where every believer can find their place and be fruitful. The Church is God's instrument on the earth today. A church should not be a black church or a white church, not Chinese, African or European - you do not find these in scripture. Church should have in its congregation a reflection of the community it is in. If it's an all black community then an all black church would be the norm. If there are white, yellow and black people in the community then the church should reflect that. The church should include all races, ethnic peoples and social standing – an incredible plan.

WORSHIP

Davidic worship, which we looked at in the 'dynamic worship' chapter.

HOLY SPIRIT

Understanding the prophetic and gifts of the spirit – again we have covered that. Of course this is not an exhaustive list but some of the key points concerning the heart of MFE.

SOULS, HARVEST AND REVIVAL

Of course I could not finish this chapter without mentioning the purpose that Jesus was sent for and commanded us also to do, and that was

> Acts 16:15 "Go into all the world and preach the good news to all creation".

Why are we here? To worship the Lord – and our purpose is to make other worshippers out of those who do not know Jesus but were created to worship Him. Gifts are not to make us look good on the platform but to equip the Church to make it strong and to fulfil its purpose, which is to bring men back to God through Jesus.

Men really like titles - Apostle, Prophet, Teacher, Pastor - Jesus referred to titles in Matt 23:6-12 -men calling themselves Father, Rabbi or Teacher. Jesus just said, "Do not be called these titles". Pastor! Prophet! Or Apostle Smith! These were meant to be the description or function, not the title.

So if we are an Ephesians 4 ministry then it should be first a soul winner then Apostle – a soul winner then a Prophet – a soul winner then a Teacher – a soul winner then a Pastor, a soul winner - then all of these giftings bring revival. And what is revival? It's every Sunday, every meeting, every gathering when one or more responds to the greatest news of the Gospel of Jesus Christ – giving their lives to Jesus – being saved, repenting, turning away from sin – whatever you want to call it. This is revival. Not just having a good time by ourselves, but celebrating when souls repent. There is no greater joy than when you lead men to Jesus Christ, so the heart of MFE is to go into the entire world and preach the good news to all creation.

NOW THAT'S A LIFE WORTH LIVING!